AF251897

ANN ELIZA BLEECKER

An Anthology in Memoriam (1752-1783)

Edited By M. Myers

ANN ELIZA BLEECKER
An Anthology in Memoriam (1752-1783)

Edited by M. Myers

The cover illustration of Ann Eliza Bleecker has been done for
the Memorial Anthology of Poetry Series by local artist, Wendy
Jo Martin, Elkhart, Indiana. A freelance artist with a portfolio
of art with national recognition and acclaim. Her specialties
include: signs, murals, window painting, sculpture, logos, set
design and scenic painting for T.V., film and stage. A sample of
her work can be seen in the movie "Prancer".

Bristol Banner Books
P.O. Box 1219
Bristol, IN   46507

Proofread by Marci Westreich

Library of Congress Catalog Card Number

93-071851

ISBN 1-879183-21-8 paperback

APPRECIATION

Ann Eliza (Schuyler) Bleecker was born in October 1752, the youngest child of Brandt Schuyler and Margareta (Van Wyck) Schuyler. With one brother and two sisters, Ann was brought up in comfort and culture as her father's was one of the most aristocratic families in the colony. She had a love of reading as a child and while still young began to write creditable verse. These early poems were gay and fanciful. She married in March 1769, to John J. Bleecker of New Rochelle, New York.

Mr. Bleecker took his family to Tomhanick, a frontier village, where he "built him a house on a little eminence, which commanded a pleasing prospect" of orchard, meadow, stream, and hill.

During the revolutionary war Mrs. Bleeckers life was amassed of varied bereavements, which slowly undermined her delicate constitution. Many of her later poems appeared in "New York Magazine." These later works were "Her Graver Poems" suggested by her family problems, called by some "melancholy productions."

Mrs. Margaretta V. Faugeres made a posthumous collection of her mother's poems, stories, and pleasant correspondence, to which she prefixed a biographical sketch of the author. It was published in 1793, and a second edition appeared in 1809. Mrs. Bleecker died November 23, 1783.

∞ ∞ ∞

WORKS CITED

Dictionary of American Biography.

FEAR OF DREAMING

Asleep within the subconscious trap
that performs before death, I run the
gamut of the past. Afraid to dream, I
clutch the present. The candle is lit
Water fills the dam. Agony freezes
the throat. Years rush through the mind's eye

The mirror invades. Mouths my being
creating the vision. Roberta leaps through fire
Fingers sear the ledger. I howl to the moon
O shattered adolescence! Mirrors of omniscience!

My I fights tentacles. The octopus grasps thought
Worming from creation, the moon drives Aquarius
The glow-worm shivers. A reflection of love
Image of foreign lands. My daughter Nonie, love's
Shards — Poetry dares the fates. Gives without tremor
But I am afraid to dream. I scale the future

A hawker's mouth bellies up creatures
outshouts the past. Timeless infinity interprets
the sun. Deep in the universe, poets cling to
a chariot. Lip rhythmic tomes. Seed the earth
See with melancholy. The bent of the voyager
the flight of a daughter. A departure from
states charters by mind the myriad rivers' bind

Marnie K. Adler
Beverly Hills, FL

JOHN HARRIS McGEE III
"A good husband, a loving father"
(Epitaph poem, Spoon River style)

"He was born on February 14th,
and she named him Valentine,"
my best friend sent word.
I did love her;
but I was John Harris McGee III
of Yancyville,
and she lived in Shanty-town
just across the state line.
So I left town when she told me,
knowing her brothers would force a wedding.

I worked in my uncle's store
in Ohio for three years;
then returned home with a wife —
a girl of my own class.
She was a good woman, a good mother,
a good wife for forty years.
Yet I never loved her wholeheartedly.

I saw Valentine once, now grown.
He was a handsome lad, my unclaimed son.
I never attempted to see his mother again.
My monument states: John Harris McGee III
"A good husband, a loving father."
My obituary praised
"A highly respected citizen of Yancyville."
Yet I never really respected myself.

Helen Thomas Allison
Memphis, TN

THE FAMILY ALBUM

Lips compressed,
Their cheeks and foreheads like the gulches
Of the lands they seek,
Their young eyes stare fiercely out of faces
Aged by the trek, battle, or childbirth.

Under pokebonnet, sombrero, Union or Confederate cap,
These faded ancestors in sepia-toned daguerreotype
Breathe a common defiance of sun and sudden death.
Their hands grip rifles, fans, reins, hats, or babies
As if to let go for even a moment
Would halt their ride into this red velvet album.

Their portraits are the road maps of the West—
The rivers crossed, the battles fought, the lives missed.
Their eyes meet mine with a flicker of an ancient shutter,
Awakening me from my deadened world.

Their mute faces say,
"Death's a constant saddle mate.
And the odds of a decent burial stacked.
But we're not quitters. We'll make it!"
I slowly nod and close the book gently.

Clela Allphin-Hoggatt
Reseda, CA

LOVE KNOWS NO BOUNDS

If we were all told the same story,
to some of us it would fall on deaf ears.
If we all listened to the same news that was not so good,
only some of us would be reduced to tears.
If someone yelled "nigger", many of a
black race would rise
If a person did something spectacular, he
may be hailed by some to be above "man size".
If someone screamed "Fire" in a crowded room,
though not seeing fire, some if not all would leave
out of instant fear for the worst to happen,
believing the screamer not to deceive.
There's a right way and a wrong way, a good
and a bad way to be
An either/or, yes or no, you either
agree or you disagree.
There's a whole people dying before us of a
deadly disease and we are divided on whether
they should be treated harsh or with compassionate ease.
AIDS nor its virus has no judgement about whether one
is black or white and it doesn't matter whether we
feel it's wrong or whether we feel its right.
There's no one neighborhood it visits and it doesn't
care if you're straight or gay nor is it concerned about
the year, the month, or even the day.
It is a disease and its not divided about who it comes
to see.
It's not racist, sexist, or homophobic so why should we be.
It's not overwhelmed by those who have and those who
have not
and it doesn't give a damn whether you have nothing
or whether you have a lot.

Bummi N. Anderson
Albany, GA

COURTYARD SCENE

Amidst our stony limestone walls
    The winter lumbers in
Announced by lightning near the dawn
    While snowfall feathers thin.

A breathless sight, so rich to see
    As roofs mount high with white
Yet calm and peaceful like a sleep
    While dawn breathes forth from night.

The frosty winds swirl round and round
    Our Lady's shrine set deep
A paradox amidst the calm
    Some swirling spirits' sweep.

The little trees blow with the blow
    And humbly lend their twigs
To dress in lacy holiday
    To sway with nature's jig.

See what I have done for you
    Within the night's slow watch
The gift of dawn, white tumbling breaks
    A vision near while yet far off.

Sister Mary Regina of the Angels, O.P.
West Springfield, MA

I WISH WE HAD LOVE EVERY DAY OF THE YEAR

I wish we had love every day of the year
             then you and I would never fear the madness in the world
Our hearts would reach out to those in need all over
             the globe
for we'd fill our minds with love every day

Don't give up
remember love is the purest strength of all
and of course it's hidden right inside of you
So start looking for love in the crevices of time inside
             and I'm sure you'll succeed finding love

I wish we had love every day of the year
             then we'd see true development in the whole human race
Our weaknesses would disappear with knowledge deep inside
             and we wouldn't need to hide from ourselves

Before you can love you must find love inside
             and a metamorphosis will occur everywhere you go
So start looking for love in the crevices of time inside
             and I'm sure you'll succeed finding love

I wish we had love every day of the year
             then life would be tranquil for everyone of us
We'd have time to pay attention to the energies inside
             and we'd begin to love our neighbors as ourselves.

Joyce Andrea
New York, NY

TIME

Time, singularly within itself
Is a figment of the imagination
Distinguished from the qualitative purity
          of air, fire, water and earth.
Purity, true to form and bold
No blemish defaces its flawless mold.
As it rambles on through its worldly pace
masterfully, never lost in space.
Forever scheming in silence, holding vigil
It wings with the wind, drowns in the storm
Freezes in winter, sunning for warmth.
Time is morning, night and noon
Hovers o'er the sandy dune.
It stands in the shade, withstands the sun
Never knows when day is done.
Time never knows a breeze or calm
It goes right on sailing, it rings no alarm.
Time is morning, noon and night
Reaches depths, eternal height.
Time is all knowing, can never tell
If there is a heaven or a hell
Time is night and noon and morning
Time laughs and cries without warning.
Time, like the zephyr winds put to a test
Discerning tranquil serenity in its galactic
          nest.

Sylvia Argow
Bronx, NY

MYSTERY OF WAPSBOURNE MANOR**

Our of Fletching, down through Sheffield Park, East Sussex,
The proper English Lane turns off to Wapsbourne Manor.
Land deeds from 1100 A.D. granted to Earls of Warren, King John,
Queen Edith, in time of Edward the Confessor; named the River,
Blackbrooke and these fields, Pipers Meade, Marletts Cripsee,
Bordering meadow and wood, Holliswish. Now beyond the sun-mist,
Above the tree-lined road, we glimpse the six great chimneys
Lording the manor, planted solidly upon its Green:
          WAPSBOURNE.

Scent of boxwood heavy on the morning air, twines the ages as
Tudor windows sentry hunting fields of Kings and feudal Lords.
Old Alpha lunbers through the grand oak door. Stafford, just
behind, calling to Beatrice and Alice for a game of Cricket.

Parish of Chailey, moated Wapyilsborne: promise for persecuted
Priests; hunted, hidden in the secret chapel chamber 'neath the
Eaves; up the twisted stair, safe now behind heavy ironwork
                bolts and bars.

The Guest Room welcomes. Broad planked oak floor stretches
Lovingly to its giant fireplace: faded brick, smoked, secure.
The Highbed says, "This wall of Tudor windows will keep you from
Me, even after dusk falls upon the fields and stars keep watch."

Now in this June of '93, the kitchen's twelfth century beams,
Stare down upon a rosy English lass and Midwest matron Yank;
Sharing tea, strawberries and cream in the cool and mystery.
Two generations, two countries, seven centuries bridged within
                these ancient Manor walls today.

Bette Armstrong
Overland Park, KS

**One of a few of the small Manor Houses left in England today. Its owners Paul and
Jean Cragg, are restoring Wapsbourne.

HESYCHIA

House of peace and rest
    House of prayer
Its windows open
    to the beauty of nature
            green grass
            wild flowers
            hills
            mountains
            blue sky
            clouds
            rain
            sun
            bluebirds
            crows
            road runners
            towhees
All reveal
the beauty and glory
        of God.

Rose Ashour
Ft. Smith, AR

WHEN JUDITH SANG

No prima donna, she, no opera star,
Not state— or nation-known, just in our town,
But when she sang she carried us to far
Dim lands across the sea, the hills of brown,
The dreamless sleep of Bethlehem. Or Erin's wiles:
"I'll Take You Home Again, Kathleen," or Scotland's lakes
Of bonnie blue in Annie Laurie's isles.
Nostalgia of her tender voice still aches
In lullabyes like "Sleep, My Love," along
The hallways of the heart. I see the fjords
Of Norway's mystic heights in "Solveig's Song"—
"This Is My Land," in soaring, golden words.

Our flag waved over us without one stain
Each glorious Fourth, unfurled within her throat,
And every year she sang the song again
Which brought us up lump-throated on the note,
Our hands upon our hearts, allegiance pledged
With sober earnestness, our lives anew.
Her joyous songs were lilted, laughter-edged.
She broke our hearts with "Willow-Grey and Blue."

And when she sang belief the liquid fire
She poured converted us. "Oh, Holy Night,"
And we were there in truth. Some heavenly choir
Must claim our Judith, singing in His sight.

Alice Morrey Bailey
Salt Lake City, UT

BIRCH SEQUENCE

Birch tree, cloud-barked
banked against moving clouds
light and shadow leaves leaving
staying
flicked aside
and springing back

peach-bloom clouds
orange immovable sky
an inch of leaves
the whole tree now

        unpickable peaces
        hung on pale branches

Remembering young Frost
swinging birches
earth to sky and
back to earth, world I have
gigantic arcs left to ride
my breeze stirring up
coals of sunset
jostling snowy clouds

until I let myself finally down
        changed.

Claire J. Baker
San Pablo, CA

A WILD LIFE

These ponderous beasts that hulk along
in unrelenting countries of light,
that move on legs too thick to make
sense and should be rooted, though
that's their unarguable nature,
will stand seven days over a companion
who's passing through savanna dust,
or pass a found bone trunk to trunk,
as if they remember a fond moment,
and are reported even to tear,
as if they understand the weight
of their presence, or lack, or ours,
though we want a corner on grief.

Hyena and vulture are the teeth
and beaks of errant theories that hunger
the inevitable; the redistribution.
Economics, a carnal knowledge, so swarm
and flock, herd and school, ignore
a singular deficit, and quickly turn
back to graze and fly, to produce
another wonder.

But this beast waits all the more,
and nevertheless, and its preponderance
colors the heart, sways pachyderm
opinions against the subduing endeavor,
the trophy profit, the stolen harvest,
the ivory's deathly sculpting.

There are beasts that defy probability:
proboscidean, they slurp and trumpet
their extensions, snorkel rivers,
hail dust and nozzle water, intertwine,
that will stand a vigilant seven days
over bones spreading gravely everywhere.

Walter Bargen
Ashland, MO

A THROW AWAY KID

I feel like a yo-yo
As I bounce to and fro
To Dad then to Mom
Back and forth I go

Shall I love Mom?
Or shall I love Dad?
They are the only parents
That I had

I do love Mom
And I do love Dad
All that does
Is make me sad

I'm the lost luggage
Of a Mom and a Dad
Who can't stand each other
No peace to be had

This piece of lost luggage
Grows taller and yet
There's more and more
I want to forget

I wish I were back
In my baby days
When Mommy and Daddy
Were pleased with my ways

I'm divided between them
Now, what shall I do?
The anger is mounting
My life can't be through

I'll be the best
That I can be
In spite of all
The grief I see

The grief I feel
Deep in my heart
Will only grow
Each time we part

Dorothy M. Barkin
Pittsburgh, PA

UNIVERSAL MUSIC
(Written upon hearing the choral concert by the
Chancel Choir of Blankanese, Hamburg, Germany)

Voices blend.
My ears bend
To music that I hear.
Organ's sound
Roof to ground
With music that is dear!

Many voices
Here from Hamburg
Sing out joyously.
German, Russian, Frenchman, Pole
What encompasses the whole?
Music of the soul.

Merle Ray Beckwith
Santa Barbara, CA

SLEEPING UNDER THE STARS

Like flowers in sunny spring,
Star shells bloomed beneath the moon.
Tears collected in some homesick eyes.
Memories replaced prolonged miseries:
Cool grass lazed upon on the family farm—
No stretcher in sub-zero Stalingrad*—
Stars that shepherded boyhood shenanigans—
Not flares above frozen forms beyond
      a field hospital.

Richard F. Bell
Marquette, MI

*Without medical supplies many of the critically wounded were left outside for euthanasia.

THE MUSIC OF THE NIGHT

The music of the night
that is what you sing.
You sing with your heart
and not with your mind, or time.
Sometimes I wish that gift was mine.
You have mastered the talent, so divine!

That voice, so strong, so deep,
yet gentle and sweet.
I wonder, do you know
how your music moves me so?
I feel as though I am the
only person in the room.
When you sing your heart out so true
I feel as though I am experiencing
something new, almost like a
new invention without infection.

Your passion for the music
makes me feel so alive.
So alive that I almost want to cry.
I believe that you as a person are one.
You don't act for people,
you, and the music are one.
Your soul is the music and
the music, is very much you.

You are the song in my heart
and the sun in my day.
I really don't know what else to say.
You make the music come alive,
you do that in such a way
that I almost want to die.
I sometimes feel like I am
experiencing something new like
...........the music of the night.

Tonya Ann Bergstad
Minot, ND

HAIKU FOR A LAST WALTZ

October roses
flaunt June remembered hues to
dance with first frost. Wilt.

Kathryn Boice
Richland, WA

AUGMENTATION

If i could reach out to someone in this life
with faithful devotion
so thick and so true—
i could be relaxed in knowing
i have changed all i once knew,
and therefore,
i will have successfully
made a difference.

Nicole Borelli
Bensalem, PA

EYES

"The eyes are the windows to the soul."

She was heavy-set, dressed in the attire
        of many today—

Blue jeans, a visored cap,
Nothing feminine about her appearance

But when she turned and spoke to me
There was so much purity, honesty
        and beauty in her eyes,

It was as if I were in the presence
        of an angel.

                                        Betty Jean Borland
                                        Washington, D.C.

QUESTING

Into quiet, hush and calm
the Radiant Azure Blue
dissolves the cluttered clutch
sweeps stillness to the heart
        A resting

In that revered serenity
can tranquility be a test
and motionlessness persue?
Yes. Radiance suggests such
        A questing

B. J. Bramhall
Morristown, NJ

GERONIMO

The terror in the face,
terror of the face

lost love, a lost love,
love lost, a love lost

ev'rmore, altogether,
lost, f'rever

'n what, what what what now?
now, after all?

David Branco
Fairhaven, MA

DECEMBER: SMALL PROMISES

the roses are shrivelled, burned by the cold
and I fear they cannot bloom again
I mourn the death of my garden
now a stick garden
trees and bushes casting linear shadows

except for the holly
except for the shasta daisies
which took possession of the flower bed
stubbornly green and supple
I pull up the dahlias
shaking soil from the thick tubers
and cut back the chrysanthemums
releasing their fragrance
with each snip of the clippers

there are two sparrows on the fence
their feathers puffed into fat little balls
I want to bring the birds closer to the house
I'd welcome them to fly through my rooms
and nest at the top of the stairs
but I am shy and they are shy

I make the rounds of my garden
and notice the three o'clock sun
highlighting small knobs of growth
on the peach tree
the forsythia is thick with buds
waiting to burst into a blaze of yellow
and the branches of the crab apple tree
are alive with small promises

Betty Bressi
Staten Island, NY

THEIR SECOND SPRING

At first transplanting, our gentle pansies
Droop and sag, no longer pulled heavenward.
Through the long, cool evening they faint,
Appearing to be lost and unable
Either to return or to continue;
But, when the morning dew begins its work,
A surge of life passes into their stems,
Even into roots hidden deep below;
While the tips of the pansies' leaves reach out
To accept the grasp of the sun's first rays,
Securely, in the growing warmth of life,
Lifted from clutches of the damp soil,
Ready to return to a better life
In a new, more congenial surrounding
Specially prepared by a Gardener
Who knows their every need and glory.

John F. Britt
Kettering, OH

FOREST

Life is a forest—
Thick heavy trees
provide shade
and help hide
problems
The colors of all
the flowers and plants
display the different
highs and lows
that one experiences
The different trails
show the many paths
that one can choose from
to carry out
their life
The vastness shows
life's journey and
how it can last long
The sudden dead ends
show the unexpected
twists and turns one
must face
Life is a forest
you can start anywhere
and see where it
will take you—
but one must be
careful—
not to get lost.

Donna Marie Bucko
Darien, IL

AUTUMN ORIGINALS

October makes a fashion statement. Gone
Are summer florals. Now an atmosphere
Of pageantry propels the waning year
Down byways edged with weedy hangers-on;
And I, like any autumn myridon,
Traverse these roads ignoring things austere,
To glimpse the woodland glory far and near
Where leaves reflect a season's benison.

Lest lack of contrast sacrifice this chic
When colors reproduced a thousandfold,
Burst forth in scarlet, bronze and shades between—
It's tempered at the height of its mystique
When sugar maple flame and aspen gold
Accessorize with shades of evergreen.

Rose Winters Burns
Canada

EPITAPH

I am sleeping, here, on this bleak hillside
Where water don't stand and horney toads hide;
To live on ants and shoot blood from their eyes
At any threatening critter that passes by.
The desert owl sleeps in the prairie dog's nest.
In peaceful habitation, they lay down to rest.
The wild coyote sings a lullaby,
As the restless breeze goes drifting by.
The Yucca, God's Candles, will bloom so white.
Their radiant glow lights up the night.
Countless stars twinkle in Heaven's dome
Until Jesus comes to call me Home.

Virginia Stonestreet Bush
Roswell, NM

IT IS MARCH AND THE COLTSFOOT IS LATE

Our house warms through continuous
chinese whispers, questions, quizzes,
endless crosswords, quixotic attempts
to engage the neighbours in conversation.

Melancholy hovers, descending hawk-like.
We change beds nightly, speak of spaces.
Blossom comes quick, voicing below words
unseen movements that rise and fall.

Clouds hang around with stunned faces.
Cohesion fades. We all ignore strangers.
Paraffin clings to the air.
Our spirit binds like bailer twine.

Snow flurries excite. Children rub each
other, nudge horizons. Bluebells stick
out spiky hints. Black-caps skim.
Each wing a cutting edge.

To live as a Great Spotted Woodpecker,
catching at an unstable bliss. Cures,
trails leading nowhere, with no one
to explain. A shrinking dot disappearing.

Clarity of far white sky. vivacity
of the morning kiss, waving goodbye
to the girls as they set off for school.
It is March and there is so much to come.

David Caddy
England

ON DEATH AND DYING

It isn't death that frightens me,
It isn't death that challenges me.
It isn't death that I resist,
It isn't death that I regret.
It isn't death that I'm mad about,
It isn't death that I'm sad about.
It isn't death that I can't face.
It isn't death that I can't tolerate,
It isn't death that I want to escape,
It isn't death that I even hate.

But what about DYING?

It's dying that I want to wait,
It's dying that, indeed, I hate.
It's dying that makes me cry,
It's dying that I want to know: why?
It's dying that's no fun,
It's dying that makes me want to run.
It's dying that gives me pain,
It's dying that seems in vain.
It's dying that I feel such shame,
It's dying that makes me insane.

And yet,

It's dying that we must all someday claim,
in spite of Pain.

Kimberly Caldwell
Culver City, CA

ZOOT SUIT

To my recollection
We never played catch
He never took me camping
He never took me fishing
He never taught me how to play chess
We never even went to the zoo

But we did go to a lot of freak shows together
Me in my baseball cap
And him in that lime green zoot suit

He loved that zoot suit

We went to freak shows all the time
We'd gawk at the pinheads
We'd glance at the hideously deformed snake man
We'd cringe as the geek bit off the head of a live chicken
For a bottle of booze
We'd watch in amazement as the limbless hot dog man
Would roll a cigarette with his mouth and light it
With his tongue
We'd gasp at the man with the bottom half of his writhing
Twin sticking out of his chest
We'd stare at the repulsive dog-faced girl
The monstrous pig boy, horror upon horror
But it was meant to teach me a lesson

When we would leave the freak shows, my father would
Put his arm around me and say,
"Son, as you go through life and you think you have problems
Just remember these poor bastards and their problems"

And I thought to myself, yeah, they got problems, real problems,

But at least they don't have to be seen in public
With a guy in a lime green zoot suit

Howard Camner
Miami, FL

WHEN COMES THE TIME

When comes the time that what boys hoped
Becomes what foolish men had dreamed,
And destinies for which they groped
Dim through darkened backdoor screens,
Where in the dying of the light
They wonder where their lives went wrong
To leave them to this summer night
And the cricket's song?

When comes the day that what men dreamed
Comes back as shameful innocence —
Before they learn the worldly schemes
And after dreams make so much sense —
When never more will they believe
That dreams bear men for men who long,
But stand in silence, there to grieve
This summer night, and the cricket's song?

When comes the night that dreams awake
Men who slept their lives away,
And bleary-eyed, for old time's sake
They rise and go from where they lay:
Where, staring back through darkened doors
They listen to the countless throng
Of loves and hopes, the unfought wars
Beyond this night and the cricket's song?

Then comes the time that they return
To lie where most men choose to lie,
Despite the shameful hopes that burn,
The unfought wars that never die;
And there, clear-eyed upon their bed
They hear what they heard all along:
The hopeful boy they loved is dead
In the cricket's song.

Christopher Carlisle
Amherst, MA

THE RETURN

In this mean time
I walked across
the map of a life
on patterned bricks
past the lightning-grooved
bark of a pine
looking for a lost name
and the field's rough
in the days of naming.

In this mean time
between an eroding road
and a home's white boards
in a shaft of morning
I glimpsed a tracing
of the way to go
and leaving the season
that gave what it could
I leaned around
toward voices I knew
to astonish me
as in the beginning.

Bernadette Carlson
Spokane, WA

MILKY WAY BLUES

I don't know nothin about the blues
but I'm gonna write them anyway
I'm gonna take my blues
and spread them on the Milky Way

I don't know nothin about writing
though I say I'm one
who does
I'm gonna reinvent myself
make words that say
I am
not
I was

It's dangerous to write
what you don't know about
but I'm going to write the blues
write them anyway
lose my don'ts
lose my was's
lose my nothings in the Milky Way

Milky Way Blues

Wil Carter
East Point, GA

FLARE FIRE

When the trip flares
went off the night sky
lit up like a baseball
field You could count
the pairs of bone chilling
jungle eyes before you
pulled the trigger—
lobbed the mortar rounds
into the short haired
grass before the rounds
went in and the slicing
fire followed

Ray Catina
Schenectady, NY

E A POE, ELECTION DAY, THE LAST OF HIS LIFE

The last visitation was by Christ reading an apocalyptic
        Vision, five
Stallions illuminated by a million lights that defied
        seeing.
Blinded, I reeled, immobilized by a sense of internal
        agony that tears me apart.
I hear sirens; mythical and real, calling out from the
        streets of and alleyways of
Baltimore.

What a place to achieve such illumination!

I am moved to continue seeking salvation from the sagging,
        drooping tit of reason.
May the tit continue to leak Remy Martin and may the
        illusion of succor keep me
From these night visions of unspeakable horror that is
        my life.
Even now, close to the source of language, fire inhabits
        my veins; a galaxy of suppurations
Implodes behind my eyes.
I am naked again with all the dead women of my life.
I will never make love or vote in Baltimore again.

Alan Catlin
Schenectady, NY

LOVE TO THE FULLEST

Love to the fullest once roamed our earth,
He arrived here by means of a heavenly birth.

From the very beginning most everyone knew,
There was something so special this child
Would do.

As time would prevail he became a man,
Teaching us love from Gods own hand.

Though to some he knew he would be such a
Dread, they never could rest until he was
Dead.

He knew his own fate from beginning to end,
He knew and still loved his betraying friend.

He carried his cross upon his two feet, to
Die for our sins and our total defeat.

Why did he do it? No reason, but love.

He wanted to help us to heaven above.

Who was this man with such merciful love?
None other than Jesus, our savior above!

Patricia Cisco
Wenonah, NJ

INDIANA BLUES
(For Vanessa, Kendra, Angie, and Group 20)

Envelopes come bearing
colors of the world. Friends
long ago and far away.

Stamps, showing regret, and
despair, previous owners expressed
grief for the missing members of
distant memories,
Trying to remember....remember.

Of times gone by.... Carefree
recreation and good times
shared with each other.
No one realized that time
had other plans.

Letters about the Queen, koalas,
the Kansas plains, college, soccer,
These adorn my walls, trying
to return to my friends,
        my hopes,
        my dreams,
        in Indiana.

I miss you, write again soon.

Corey Clayton
Sharpsville, PA

NATURE'S DAWN

Morning emerges
Shocked by its illumination as
Lighted day spurns obscurity
And envelops distant horizons

Rising from slumber, some appealing
Grapplers breathe in conscious breathe
While other small beings compete
For some nectar or prey
Among brush and thicket

A nocturnal dweller closes eyes
And resigns enticed for his
Daily repose whistling and
Rousing a few of the lazy and intractable

Time flourishes as
A radiant sun warms the unbounded reaches,
An unrelenting origin of fiery rage
Only the heavens can cherish

Stephen Clements
Binghamton, NY

AUTUMN LEAVES

Goldenbrown are the leaves
they've lived their life upon the trees

Autumn's here life soon shall pass
their valt lies upon the grass

Live's lived A purpose done

EULOGY

The wind and setting sun

Dale Cody
Indianapolis, IN

AT THE JAPANESE TEA GARDEN

My heart is burning for my love.
I wonder what she's doing now.
Her trickster smile,
poised at an angular
backward glance.
Her head down.
Her ebony black hair
urging me to catch her.
How she stares at me,
tempting, taunting too:
    come back.
Staring out of the rocks,
Hovering in the air.

Jim Cody
El Paso, TX

MISS MANDY
(Amanda Burk Blocker. Texas Cattle queen)

She was lovely and blonde, a sweet South Texas belle
　　but, inside, she was tough as a boot.
She was wed to Bill Blocker, a cattleman king,
　　had a sixgun and knew how to shoot.

One day, Big Bill set out on a huge cattle drive
　　herding one thousand wild Texas steers
To the Red River Valley, far up in the North
　　and his lady was left home in tears.

So Miss Mandy took after the herd by herself
　　with a buggy and a two-pony team
And she raced it along, up that rough cattle trail
　　over sandbank and gully and stream.

Miss Mandy could drive like a charioteer;
　　before long, she caught up with her man.
All the way to the Red River Valley, up North
　　Mandy followed that steer caravan.

Sometimes, cowboys sing songs that will quiet their herds,
　　keeping watch over them through the night
But a bright flash of light or a loud thunderclap
　　can excite them to stampede in fright.

On the prairie, one night, such a downpour occurred—
　　Blocker's herd took off over the plain
So Bill placed his poor, frightened wife under a tree
　　and he left her alone in the rain.

With the dawn, when the stampede had quieted down
　　and her husband was finally free
She stood, shivering, waiting there, drenched by the rain
　　with her ponies' ropes tied to the tree.

Many sagas are dung about pioneer men
　　who led bold and adventurous lives
But we seldom hear praise of the valor, the strength
　　and the courage of pioneer wives.

So, I'll sing you a song of a pioneer belle—
　　one who carried a six-shooter handy.
One who trail herded steers with a buggy and team;
　　out in Texas they called her Miss Mandy.

Eddie-Lou Cole
Sacramento, CA

DEATH SENTENCE
(My doctor said)

"I just can't promise you a year."
My heart was overwhelmed with fear.
I know how quickly time will fly,
and, really, I don't want to die!

Then reason came to calm my fear.
No one is promised another year.
Today is all that we can claim,
tho' future days we wish to gain.
So make the best of now—today,
then if you see another dawn,
Thank God for what He's given you
and find some worthwhile task to do.

Don't sit around and mourn and sigh,
don't grieve that someday you may die.
Of course you will—so shall we all
when e'er we hear the Masters call.
Each life on earth is in His Hand.
Each goes according to His plan.
Man came from Him—To Him returned.
I praise the Lord for what I've learned.

What future could be half so fair
as what awaits my soul up there?
Thank You, Dear Lord, for promise given.
That I shall have a place in Heaven.

Patti Cordell
Flora Vista, NM

THE SCREEN
(Cambridge MA: September 1, 1966)

Left by a bourgeois Progressive Laborite,
         this delicate screen
freezes flora & fauna as they fall
            in a Japanese early Autumn,
         butterflies & leaves
in stages of progressive evolution,
         all progress hieratic.

         Imagine what effort
for his mind & the mind of its maker,
            to tamper with nature
for art's sake, principle & convictions
         the price of possession.

         Radical truth curses
possessors turned progressive with
   "You can only want things for others"
         while Joan & I,
educated working-class children,
         sit, its current owners
by cultural dissociation & default.

         What is its value?
Not itself; instead, its provocation,
         arresting nature
with man's most natural process,
         transformation.

         Outside our window,
chilling flora & fauna stand in
         New England's early Autumn
as the screen of our minds reflects.

                                        Bill Costley
                                        Wellesley, MA

SEASONS

The passions of the winds in springtime,
Torrid air of summer days,
Unleashed beauty rampant in autumn,
Winter's cold and snowy haze...
Seasons bow to Nature's bidding,
Each to bring about its course;
From scenes of flowers gently nodding,
To winter's closing of all doors.
Life continues in its seasons,
Age to age and year on year;
Knowledge, wisdom, mindful reason...
Not all mysteries made clear.

Phyllis Crago
Prairie Village, KS

I HAVE CLIMBED A HUNDRED HILLS

I have climbed a hundred hills—
I have seen mallards drifting
    on the water crest
And an opal sky
    in the dawn.
Dew on forget-me-nots,
    a spider's web silver in the sun,
    fragments of a rainbow after rain.
I have heard
Holy things, music, prayer, love's voice,
    age old hymns,
        cathedral chimes,
Strains of immortal Ave Maria.
I have paused beside an iris blossom,
    blue as the Madonna's robe,
And knelt in the silence of temple altars.
I have touched a baby's satin cheek,
    velvet softness of rose petals,
        cool sculptured marble,
silky strands of golden tasseled corn,
    and a friendly hand.
I have listened to budding prayer—
    a child's first prayer.
I know a love that blossomed
    as a white magnolia tree
    by a garden wall.
A sinking sun, a red sun,
    a gold sun is going down
        behind the hills
            at God's behest.

Emma Crobaugh
Highland Beach, FL

REVERIE OF ANOTHER DAY

Processions gliding in phases of movement,
And stillness through my window, like woven
Murals; now sheets of whims of children—
Hustle branches, and sway sadnesses, on
My tree,- like dancing ladies, too secret
For judgment, piercing silences—
Known when no answer came. My eyesight
Anchored in the sea of my life's entries
In the book of dreams. In my corner,
Musing the knights' songs - stale
Questionings, bothering with duty, a mind
Awed, and trying to relent.

No boast to govern his soul
These small friends, and dancers, and knights
Are in control

Little of the day regarded in its
Assumptions

He is lonely for the extravagances
Lent from time's life - lifting the
Strange pale believers to the brotherhood
Of extending their wits, through fleeting
Surmises, happy to amend.

Arthur Croe
Niagara Falls, NY

AWAITING A SUNSTORM

I can handle the death of my dreams.
I can't stand the loss of another's...
All those songs unsung, the kisses unkissed,
The promises faded by silence.
Late nights can echo with words long unheard.
Mornings can beg for a sunstorm.
I can live with the end of my dreams.
Or, maybe, they breathe after all!

Linda Lee Curtis
Phoenix, AZ

THE SEARCH

One is touched
            with melancholy
remembering the little things
that brightened up sad lives
            long ago—

The desperate clinging
to a passing happy moment
when cares were gone.
The search for meaning
in random suffering
hoping for relief
for the innocent victim
throughout the endless years.

And at last release
and for those observing
finally consolation.

Mary Louise Curtis
Pensacola, FL

IT IS LOVE

it is warm
it is moist and dark
it moves like wind on silk
it has high red cheeks
and sweat on its brow

eyes closed lightly
lips parted slightly
movement
imperceptible—almost

then more
a great shaking
something
awaking!

then slow and soft and gentle and warm;
breathing great gasps
hot air
cool skin
slide swerve slip   shhhhh

it is warm

it is love

Jeff Custer
San Francisco, CA

THE SECOND WIFE SPEAKS

The one time I saw Her we were all on a picnic
By a sandy stretch of the Ninnescah.
She huddled against the sand like a nesting bird,
Her clothes like drooping feathers on Her bones.
Death loured in the hollows of Her parchment face.
Her children darted like hummingbirds
Bringing Her treasures—
Marbled pebbles, runic twig shapes, ravaged shells.
They swooped and swirled and did not wait to see
How brief the smile their largesse summoned.
And he was there, crisp and sunny as autumn morning,
His body sparking with life,
His white shirt sweaty, sleeves rolled up, collar open.
Had She somehow managed to iron that shirt, I wondered.
Did the soggy ruin of Her work bring on that look of mild dismay?
He sheltered Her with smiles
Or for a moment curved his bronzed arm
Like an angel pinion around Her sagging shoulders.
Then the game called and back he dashed
To laughter, strife, victory,
With just one quick look back.

Now I'm making a small garment.
It is white and soft as breath.
I'll trim it with pink embroidery.
The treadle of Her sewing machine
Looks lacy, but it is iron, black and cold.
My foot more than covers the spot
Worn shiny by Her treading.
I push against it. Hard.
Her children perch around me.
Their big eyes and small voices
Pat me on the head as if I were the child.
Polite and pensive as old owls,
They bring me nothing.

Julia Dagenais
Wichita, KS

WHEN WE'RE APART
(for Dave)

Look to the stars
When you feel alone,
And know I am there
And you're never alone.

Whisper my name,
And I'll answer your heart,
Because in our hearts
We're never apart.

Savor the wind
As my warm embrace.
The rain as my kiss
Adorning your face.

My smile is the sunlight,
My tears are the dew.
So remember forever,
I'm *always* with you!

Julia Ann David
West Middlesex, PA

MIND AND THE EYE

The bridge arches
  over a river
    flowing beyond
      the eye,
        and a bird
          curves
            into realm
of song, but mind
  and the eye
    follow
      wing of bird
        until space
          where the bird
            has been
              beckons
                dawn. The eye
returns to arc
  of bridge
    and light on
      stone, yet
        mind contemplates
          marvel of
            bird and
round of bridge
  until bridge and
    stone and bird
      and eye become
        being and
          feeling
            and ever one.

Irene Dayton
E. Flat Rock, NC

FRAGILE CRAFT

Up, up, in the sky
a mosquito-like
plane flies.
Wings, thin and fragile
held together with
spun wire.
A tiny motor hums steadily.

Life travels
tremulously in this
light-weight craft.
Temptations and storms
test our small
machine.
May we not lose
altitude or,
worse yet,
crash!

S. June Desmond
Fond du Lac, WI

SEARCH FOR BEAUTY

Lovers of Beauty and Art
Let not your inner convictions depart.
But, rise to rebuke the trend to despoil
All the magnificent structures built with toil.

Progress? - - - - - so oft they say.
In this great city - - - - - is there no creed?

save greed?
As of old - - - - for gold?

Must I go to another land
Where reverence for Men and Beauty still stand?

Where the the Poet, the Painter, the Architect dwelt,
With pride and inspiration in what they felt.

Perhaps Florence, Venice, or Rome
As an exile, I'll find home.

Let me be a part to find heart.
Where stand Men of Stature

And a living culture—
Who do not tred under in cruel disgrace
A city of Culture, Beauty and Grace.

Alicia Devereaux
Carmel, CA

ON THE EDGE OF THE *ACEQUIA*
(*Taos, New Mexico*)

The snow's given in to the sun,
And Lee's out there pruning
The yellow rose bushes on the edge
Of the *acequia*, and I'm writing
Inside my study one poem about
A kite, and a second about
The three main differences in people.

My concentration's interrupted
Once ever few minutes when
I choose to look up from my Olympia
Through the window and out
To her with those pruning shears
Lopping away with her upper body,
Making for a more human flow
Of water across this Taos land.

I feel she's doing more important work
Than I am, at first;
                and at second,
That *I* am;
       and at third,
Why am I so happy trying to rank things?

R. P. Dickey
Ranchos de Taos, NM

COLOR PRINT

Deep sepia tones of trees in foreground
In path above blue lake at side,
Green foliage of pines in background,
Light green foliage of the grove of trees.
Along back rim of lake light blue sky above.
Coming down the shadowed sepia path
A young man in plaid shirt and gray jodphurs
Astride a brown horse with a furry dog
Following. This could be old Ireland.

Bettina Dietrich
Madison, FL

POEMS

A song that's alive
A Corvette to drive
Two peas in a pod
Some scales on a cod
A dream that keeps waking
A picture worth taking
Some seeds for sowing
A love forever growing
A beautiful picturesque sight
Memories in poems to write

Jennifer Dopkin
Richboro, PA

GUATEMALA CITY

Guatemala City is extremes,
from the little tiendas in homes
to the large shopping malls,
and from the glaring light poles
to the rutted streets.
It is short, tight skirts
on beautiful young women,
cars and buses belching opaque fumes.
It's where pock-marked walls
hide from view comfortable homes,
and gringos never imbibe the water,
Guatemala City is a five-year-old
Indian girl begging at the airport.

Margaret English
Novato, CA

HIS EYES WERE GREEN IN HOUSTON

His Eyes Were Green
In Houston
On a bus
In heat as deep as the sea-green eyes
In Houston
On a bus
Behind him, moving, the trees and grass-green eyes
In Houston
On a bus
Like a clear plastic yo-yo I had once, Imperial-green eyes
In Houston
On a bus
Glowing from his black face, laser-green eyes
In Houston
On a bus
Suddenly he stood
His children of the damned eyes
Round jade saucers,
He was led to the door
His luminescent clock hand eyes
Glowed with borrowed light green eyes
In Houston
On a bus.

J. Ferguson
Cold Spring, NY

FRIENDSHIP'S LINK

God is the anchor of our lives.
You are a vital link
In the chain.

We exist in different worlds,
Yet our prayers bond us
Together.

We are alive on this plain—
Continuing on our journey,
A course set
By one invisible.

We have no end.
The universe is ours
Forever.

Karen A. Flynn
Pittsburgh, PA

SHOWOFFS

The mushers took off at midnight from Marquette
last night on a two hundred mile race
of sleds and dogs for $25,000,
through woods, towns, and over frozen lakes.

Today the Metropolitan Museum
sent Thalia, Muse of Comedy,
by postal Express I had to get, a break,
from the back door post office workers.

With so much art surrounding me today,
and an Ethiopian hijacker
in jail in Florida and a bomber
giving up his terror in Stockholm,

it's almost easier to believe the artists'll
win the garland for showing "What is man?"

Leslie D. Foster
Marquette, MI

BEYOND EXPECTATION

I

I never thought I'd see the Shannon
Where beside Athlone it flows,
Nor yet a wee thatched cottage
Latticed with the Irish rose.

II

No more I thought enthralled to stand
In the lee of London Tower,
Nor gaze on halls of Parliament
Where Britain wielded power.

III

I never dreamed the green of Eire
To be the verdant hue it is,
Nor visioned Rome's Campagna
To be the varied view it is.

IV

Forearmed with prudent warnings,
I scaled the heights of staid Paree,
"I came, I saw" - was conquered
By Parisian courtesy.

V

Now when I treat of war and peace,
No longer far will be the cry
To the beach of Normandy
Or the Palace of Versailles.

VI

I never thought I'd see Espagna
Who gave American missions birth,
And planted her colorful culture
In our corner of the earth.

VII

When I bade adieu to Lisbon
And hailed the latest port of call,
Little I dreamed New York would seem
The city most cordial of all.

S. Mary Lawrence Franklin, RSM
Erie, PA

IN LIFE I WANDER
(In Memory of William F. Frantz IV)

In life I wander
Always looking around
Of golden dreams I often ponder
Knowing there is something that has never
been found

I look for something I think I miss
To understand people is the hardest thing
To go on with no love, no real kiss
As if no bells of hope will ring

I think of life as something unreal
Unseeing and not so nice
Coming along never to heal
With it as hot as ice

To wonder what will come
Feeling with the feel of being lost
Loneliness as if it was brung
Being there without a cost

On and on I walk on a field of past
Life is cheap and thin like a rope
But always wishing it will last
Trying to keep with the building
of hope

To put down people for the length of their hair
Stuffed up people putting you down
He's not important so treat him unfair
Running around, hearing bad sounds

William Frantz III
Lockport, NY

THE SOUNDS OF SUMMER
(31 July 93)

today the chorus of cicadas
is swelling, like some unearthly
bellows breathing, rising on one
side and subsiding around the
other, hum and drone of god's
organ in the sky, counterpointing
call of crows fading in the sky

invisible until they fall and
lie sputtering on the sidewalk,
buzzing and croaking weakly,
large black and blue oblong bugs
enshrouded in translucent wings,
some joined end to end as if
exchanging seed for offspring

these are the sounds of summer,
pervasive and brief, enveloping
the heat of our days with strange
vibrations, performance of lives
about to be harvested by the
handfuls from the sheltering trees
heavy under their August leaves,

the grass browning dryly beneath,
spinning their hearts on kazoos
of steel shaking in the breeze,
as if they could live forever,
as if *I* could live forever, singing
my heart out, fit for the journey
wherever it goes, no questions asked,

whether in the trees with their
weight of leaves, or here on the
ground littered with wings.

                Tonight
we are drenched in the swelling
of peepers, jingling absurdly like
sleighbells, steadily, until they
too fall prey to the encroaching Fall

Norman Friedman
Flushing, NY

CHAMBERED NAUTILUS
(A Painting By Andrew Wyeth)

Mega, serene, you hug
Your blanket-bent knees,
Gaze mystically through the sun
Splashed panes of the closed window
Facing the river, intent,
Listening for the ocean,
Rolling in the sound.

Nearby, a basket of trinkets,
Paper, pencils and beloved Bible
Lie ready to record or recall fond memories.
Your four poster, like rooted stumps,
Support the delicate lace-cloud canopy,
And at the foot of the bed,
A Chambered Nautilus.

Imprisoned, confined invalid,
Your quiet longing to escape
Is reminiscent of that spiraled
Mother-of-pearl that legend tells,
Outgrew itself, leaving
A perfect shaped coil
To remind us of its existence.

Lee Frisbee
Brockport, NY

MR. POSTMAN

Time is always running fast but you try to run faster
Endless complaints from customers and the nagging postmaster
House after house after street after street
Every minute of every hour you must be on your feet
Through the freezing snow and under the scorching sun
Sloshing through the rain doesn't sound like much fun
Oversized packages that never seem to fit
Being chased by dogs - large and small - hoping not to get bit
Not enough postage - incorrect zip code
Returned to sender - Addressee unknown
Cars blocking your way so receptacles won't open
Boxes filled with trash or just plain broken
You gulp down your lunch because it's time to move on
Then "Hey you can't walk there! I just fixed my lawn!"
"Where is my check? It should be here by now!"
They want it that moment and they don't care how
You may be extremely tired but you don't have time to sit
Then people quarrel over junk mail as if you wrote it
If there ever is a problem or something they just don't understand
All they ever say is "Blame it on the mailman."
You're either too early or else you are too late
For those who aren't ready or do not want to wait
Each and every day from dawn till dusk
You work so hard delivering for us
Have we ever said we appreciate all that you do?
If not, it's about time and we'd like to thank you!

Christina Frondoso
Irvine, CA

IMITATING GREAT POETS

Knife, weave, hover or dart
through the moment sky
with sinews pliant, stretched

each with your singular song or cry
— raven, nightingale, woodthrush, lark —
matching the rhythms of your heart

and where you feel the planet's pull
and strain to face the sun
I will follow you

only in the strength of my own wings
and casting my own tune.

Joan Austin Geier
Roosevelt Island, NY

RIVER REFLECTION

It's flowing motion drew me
    to that forbidden childhood place
Where I stockpiled secret time
    and listened to river-ghosts sing.
In spring I watched swollen currents
    rearrange the helpless land,
In summer I searched for clamshells
    hidden in small canyons.
When autumn's stillness turned
    burnished shores into mirrored visions,
Or winter icefields beckoned,
    except for patches of black water,
I never felt the danger then...
    when I heard the river-ghosts sing.

Joan Marie Giusto
Bradley, IL

APPLES IN THE SNOW

The old man loved the children. They could play
Inside his orchard, any time, he said.
One rule he made. That they must keep away
From his choice tree — an apple that bore red
Delicious fruit just right for jelly jar.
Its taste his drop-in neighbors long had known,
And they brought with them friends from near and far
To savour jam his favorite tree had grown.

When he passed, even children gathered round,
But as in falls to follow, no one cared
To touch this cherished fruit upon the ground
So it remained — a legend we all shared,
And many are who ask the few who know
The story of red apples in the snow.

Hazel Firth Goddard
Canada

EPITHALAMIUM

Permit an elder brother to bestow
Words of advice whose truth he cannot know:
Yet I, who've never known connubial bliss
Have known, despite, the joy of lover's kiss;
But in that kiss was more of lust than love.
Your love was made in Heaven up above,
And renders sacrament what would be sin —
A prize that I have never sought to win.
Upon your conjugation is a blessing
That renders guiltless you and your undressing
And now revered is and is cherished more.

And yet, I cannot help but think at times
Of nights I've spent in love with my own kind
That seemed so much like marriage, all I missed
Was God's name spoken on the lips I kissed.

Eugene Godilo-Godlevsky
Mt. Kisco, NY

LOVES JOURNEY THE SONG

It commenced in a much earlier time,
before the world was yours or was mine.

It trilled its way through countries and history,
some of it penned and some of it mystery.
With strength, commitment, determination and love,
always with help from the One up above.

It traversed, it journeyed to two people so young,
they loved, they had values, they lived as were one.

From their love and commitment came children, one I,
and we thrived and we learned and we laughed and we cried.
We were encompasses in love, security sweet,
we learned principles, tenderness, faith...not defeat.

We lived in that nest like new little birds,
surrounded by warmth and safety, secured.
We nourished, we absorbed, we loved and we grew,
then we gently were pushed, it was time and we knew...

How to soar, how to fly, how to rise on our wings,
how to live, how to labor, to embrace all life brings.

The journey continues, my life mate and I,
we are singing the song, the notes sailing high.
Some say we are old fashioned, but as days go by,
the good choices are made, we do not question why.

For our roots they go deep, our beliefs they are strong,
we continue our journey, we sing timeless song.

We give thanks to our parents, our families so dear,
our God and our Guide for bringing us here.
To this place in our journey of tranquility and peace,
in a world full of anger, selfishness and defeat.

We know someday our travels will end,
and we will pass on the torch, others to send.
We will go to that place of joy with such depth,
thanking all of our ancestors for fortitude kept.

So we are spreading our arms and embracing those young,
we are thrilling, for we know the song will be sung,
and a sweet rewarding new chapter in the journey begun.

Debora J. Good
Elkhart, IN

ANN ELIZA SCHUYLER BLEECKER

What a short and tragic life —
Ann Eliza Schuyler,
Born in Olde New York before the birth of the Nation;
She married John J. Bleecker at the age of seventeen
And moved to Tomhanick on the frontier upstate.

There she had two daughters, but her younger one, Abella, died
while they were fleeing British troops.
Her mother and sister died within months of each other;
Then she lost the baby that she was carrying
when her husband was captured by the British.
All this tragedy in so short a life.

As we sail on her beloved Hudson River
on a peaceful Sunday afternoon
Our blessings seem so bountiful—
in a nation not at war with other nations
we have enjoyed long and secure lives
with children and grandchildren—
What gratitude we feel toward these pioneers
who forged our inheritance through their trials.

May our children be able to know the same gratitude to us.

EmmaLeigh Goodwin
Upper Nyack, NY

LOST

The children keep
coming to the
quiet place
of no name
the whiteworld
where water runs
slick as glass
and geese rest
all settled in
under their skin
ghostsmoke
easing between
tops of trees
as birds
rehearse in pews
tracking farther
over the pale
derelict snow
repeating their heart
from memory
too soon
lost

G. Timothy Gordon
Spearfish, SD

THINGS ARE NOT ALWAYS WHAT THEY SEEM

Cumulus clouds have a clear way of saying that
    everythings's right with the world.
Most people know that these clouds often change
    to the ones from which lightning is hurled.
Children are usually innocent creatures
    but, as the years pass, can become
What those who love them have dreamed through their
    growing ... or, unlike the Prodigal Son,
"Sow their wild oats," - nor return to their fathers —
    but cherish the evil they've done.
Grapes and wild berries can promise rich harvest
    but rot on their vines in the spring.
Everything, everyone bears in himself both the good
    grain and bad ... so the thing
Wise men will search for, while asking God's guidance,
    is that they will choose the right task
(Changeless as always) in order to cultivate only
    those things that will last:
Work for the good of the people who need you but never
    expect "some return" —
These are the times for forgiving and loving, for
    striving each day to discern
Why you are here ... at this time ... in this homeland ...
    among those you meet on Life's way ...
God alone knows all the answers ... so trust Him ...
    His Son will turn night into day.

Sister Angela Clare Gorman, SP
Van Nuys, CA

STRAY

Who left it?—I have no idea
Dried up, brown, half-dead
But the little tree we nurtured
And placed in a rich bed

The fiercest wind, the deepest snow
Our sickly Stray survived
And Spring at last—we marvel
Now, it's healthy and alive

In almost every family tree
A limb bends the wrong way
It won't conform—seems steadfast
So you look the other way

But; one day you discovered
What loving care can do
Enticed the limb to grow up straight
Praised, encouraged too!

Hope with prayer to nurture
One loyal, believes, stands by
The maverick limb begins to soar
And grows straight to the sky

Helen Gougeon
Florence, MA

WEEPING WILLOW

My childhood days were spent
Along the Brandywine.
On summer days, keeping cool
Meant splashing in the Riley pool.

Tanned young bodies, around the juke box danced
To SHORT FAT FANNY and MARY LOU we pranced
To Fats Domino, and Chubby Checker, we rocked
Wet and tan, around the old jukebox.

My life has gone through many a phase
Since my innocent teenage days,
But it's hard to think of day so fine
As my days along the Brandywine

These are the days I will always miss
The park, Charlie, of that first kiss.
On life I was truly high—
I was young, tan, and full of life.

Life was fun, and not too deep,
Still, I knew time would not keep,
SO, I sat along the river,
While she swept along under the *willow*
And together, we wept
For soon that willow and me were to be uprooted.

Shirley Ann Graham
Goshen, IN

OVER THE GARAGE

I see her standing on the terrace
Yawning at the stallion-studded meadow
Gaping mouth gold at sun gold glinting back.
She scratches spewings of grayish hair,
Smudges of ashes on her silk nightgown.
I smear a dusty porthole in my window pane
To glimpse her over my dirty dishes.
What a mess with her hulking well-used flesh,
Her eyes are the only beauty trait left.
Can't hold one of those petty jobs she's had
She'll be sunning in the empty pool with gin.
This dump I live in feels outdoors all year;
The heater chugs, the water drips so loud
It's like I live downstairs in the garage.
Gave the local kids the toolshed for their club
That half-wit brother still inventing nothing,
She laughs and swerves around a Cadillac
Till her Mercedes is returned like new.
My Volks has had so many operations
If I only had a little cash for things.
These blasted poems are so hard to write—
You have to turn a spigot to get feeling.
Signatures on the walls are made by head and fists.
Why can't she see how much I need money?
The only thing she's done is charge low rent;
She seems to care only about herself.

Ray Greenblatt
Paoli, PA

OUR HOME

Our home was filled with warmth and cheer;
A nine-room house which seemed to me,
With rooms upstairs and hallways too,
A mansion of enormity.

No matter where you looked for us,
You'd find a child upstairs, below.
Eight brothers and five sisters too,
And mother and father, yet, you know.

The oldest one of course was I,
And did I ever rule that crew!
Even though today we're grown,
We still recall the times we've known.

The kitchen smelled of fresh-baked bread,
And cookies filled the platters too.
Hot cocoa steamed in thick white cups,
And mother had so much to do.

Father worked from dawn till dark,
So Sunday was a happy day;
For that was when he had the time
To take the little ones and play.

Today I look upon the past,
And bless the home we children knew;
But most of all I think of two
Whom God alone can bless anew.

Connie Guido
Arlington Hts., IL

FOR DIANE

The moon isn't white, it's ghost.
Our curtains with the ships
blow into it. Into the final settling of birds.
Our love's a conversation.
You pick it up, confident
as the brush moving through your hair,
as the cotton that lets your body breathe,
as the five creaks of the floor
before we touch—the stars coming out
in the mirror. Navigate by us they say.
Find that place where
you both lay pointing north.

Jim Handlin
Plainfield, NJ

BORNE INTO MANHOOD

Enshrouded within the clay earth,
inside a round kiva,
seven feet below the ground:
birth and death united:

An ascent, a resurrection,
as he climbed the ladder:
his eyes touched the sky —
Father,
as he planted his feet
on the plateau —
Mother.

Father and Mother greet
their son, now an adult.

The mountains are his to climb.

Paul A. Hanson
Sheboygan, WI

A MYSTICAL DREAM

I walked into the invisible
touched the intangible,
grasped wispy mists
with my now transparent hands;
found vibrations yet unknown to man.

As I floated in space,
I saw a golden glow
shimmering in light.

Its beauty brought tears to my softened eyes,
my hair bristled.

I traveled an eon of time
in one microsecond,
drank of eternity
from a gleaming goblet.

There was no beginning
no end
I was enveloped in a perfect circle.

Paul Haugh
Australia

SEASONS LOST

The Seasons came and passed
again
Since last I heard your voice.
Many are the ways I'd change
If death but gave a choice.

I'd pick you flowers in the Spring
To show you that I care
And when you needed comforting
You'd always find me there.

The Summer breeze against my
cheek
Like memories of your touch.
The love we take for granted
Is the one we miss so much.

Sunlight on the Autumn leaves,
Reflections of your hair,
Youth and beauty paid the price—
God often takes the fair.

Winter winds that chill the heart
And etch the stone with frost
Mist the tears of wasted years
For all the time we lost.

C. David Hay
Rosedale, IN

'HAPPY ANNIVERSARY'
"SUSZANNA"

Infinite chandelier of stars shining over this earth of heather jade —
Illuminating all below, with gentle beams of hope our God has made —
Here walks the earth, this lady, now sixty-two years and nine
Richly blessing the hearts of others, and now thankfully mine —
Lady of character, lady of sharing —
Lady of humility, lady of caring —
Lady of God's love for all who are to her, ever near —
This Lady of mine, with kindness and grace, so very, very dear.

Carl D. Haynes
Marion, IN

A TRANSIENT TASTE

A straight little path through golden slopes —
    Is this my way to Eternal Life?
Ah no, — no image, this, — of reality,
    Life's pilgrimage is never so!

But only this glimpse He gives to me,
    A transient taste of joy to come.
He almost speaks aloud to say
    "Just look and see your promised bliss".

Yes, I believe, my Lord, your word:
    "No eye has seen, no ear has heard";
My grateful heart rejoices now
    In what you've shown to me, to me.

Sister Mary of the Pure Heart
West Springfield, MA

BEHIND SHROUDING DREAMS

to stop meant to stay forever
leaving nothing whatsoever
on then
continue to stumble
until only hope remains
but something could be ahead
behind the vivid tapestry
the surreal majesty
of rugged sandstone mountains
separated by steep valleys
captivating the mind
to become demonic
threatening to destroy
obliterating everything
a white drifting mist appears
some substance even in that
as condensate drips from leaves
then consciousness shifts
to perceptions involving
thinning of the white shroud
allowing views of sun
with green forests below
where winds a living river
the mist thickens
darkening suddenly
and perceptions cease
until revival and sitting
feeling cool on one side
feet scuffing rock debris
water trickling from above
down a cleft opened up
in an unexpected world
dank in half dark
in the earth awaiting rebirth

Bernard Hewitt
Australia

THE FLOOD OF 93

Oh Heartland of mine
so sweet and so kind
with bountious fruits you provide
Each year is the same
Most reap and some gain
But all share God's blessing
Lest it be not in vain.
The season of spring ebbed slowly in place.
As winter reluctantly gave up the race.
The plowing and seeding were slow to arrive.
As coolness and dampness continued to thrive.
If one could surmise what ahead of us lay
All the worry and work for this year would delay.
For as summer edged closer the rains did not cease.
But came with a plunder each week with increase.
Now the creeks and the rivers engorged with the wrath
overflowed their embankments and all in their path.
Good farmland and Homesteads were put to the test
But nothing could halt the ensuing unrest
And the towns and cities by the rivers that laid.
Had their walls and levees to protect them, they prayed.
But who would have thought that these storms would prevail.
For all summer they'd had nothing but wind, rain, and hail.
Gone for a week but soon to return.
With a scorn and a vengeance like nothing they'd learned.
Now the levees that held back the torrents before
were beginning to weaken in spots shore to shore.
For in spite of the labor and sandbags and all
Nothing could salvage the crumbling well.
As the rapids burst forth and encompassed their towns
All their faces reflected their sorrows with frowns.
For who could forget all this damage you see.
And our Heartland besieged by the flood ninety-three.

Walter Hire
Middlebury, IN

A LIVING LIFE

As roaring waters
Inundate to swallow land
That has no comeback,
So life attacks, not asking
'Is one wealthy or distinguished'?
Life will terrorize, force leaving a place called home,
To find shelter where a sleeping place is just bare attic floor.
It pushes one into the strata of unsociable,
Illiterates and woebegones, even the extremes of family deaths.
Ann Eliza Bleecker, from beginning days
Shows herself to be a seeker, as mind and spirit
Rise above the gamut of the time's disturbance.
By her avid classic reading, writing her light verse,
A tension relief, as incidences touch her tender senses,
Later to be thrown right out;
Then in the throes of serious confrontation
Again she writes in overtones of frustration,
And these posthumously published, leave a nasty taste.
She a fortuitous woman, involved in conjugal devotion
Attests to high-quality personhood,
Which tells her living is greater than her works.
A woman among women! A worthy comeback on her final pack
Diffusing good smell as the years roll by.

Sister Elizabeth Hoch, F.S.P.A.
LaCrosse, WI

TOGETHER OR SEPARATELY

So much depends, yes, on some trivial, childish,
   left-behind plaything,

so much we four agreed on, making our autumnal
   great escape

in a cherry-red Olds along the edge of Lookout Mountain,
   rambling through

haze-glow, wood-smoke, pollen-cloud and midge-cloud
   but unprepared

for desperadoes leaping free as dust motes
   from a rock ledge

into golden air, encased in wires, straps, canvas, struts,
   and against body drag

a nylon cocoon to slip into, ample even to take in
   a trusting mate.

Eugene Hollahan
Decatur, GA

IN SLOW MOTION

Going on after our parting
train stopped
near Mezzovico, just like Dante
for mechanical problems
his three beasts growling
from the intercom
in German, French, Italian
promising to tell us all about it.

There was no station and the doors
stayed shut. Windows didn't open.
Outside, the wind stirred trees,
seeds floated into next spring,
swallows looping against bright clouds,
grapevines arched
their branches over signposts, crossings,
the meadows green and dripped with poppies,
snow on the mountaintops. The train moved
backwards—forwards—in sudden gasps.
Tunnel lights dimmed, the intercom
kept silent, broken. Air stopped.
Had you been there would we have spoken?

On our last night we argued—
I was difficult, and you
no comfort, though I crept
in an unsleeping moment into your arms

the light switched on in our hotelroom
so dark it darkened
sheets, our bodies
the air it fastened.

Jean Hollander
Hopewell, NJ

ON FOGGY DAYS

On foggy days, portending rain
Hangs heavy o'er the lonely lane;
    The flowers' colors fade away
    To glow more brightly on a day
When springtime sunshine comes again.

Birds sing a low and sweet refrain,
As they pick at the golden grain
    Beneath a stack of drying hay
        On foggy days.

Their songs are echoed from the plain,
As meadowlarks take up the strain;
    They give to us a note that's gay
    When early springtime's skies are grey,
And blot out all the dreary stain
        On foggy days.

Albert R. Horrell
Harvester, MO

A HYMN TO THE PLEIADES

When the Pleions began to construct
The world of form in order to receive
The Sons of the Most High into earth nature,
They formed Atlantis, a place of positive energy, with its
Arrow and chockstone ring to point away
From the Crocodile pen, symbols of greed and avarice.

Closer to energy than matter,
They beamed themselves down,
Those Shining Ones of esoteric tradition.
On Earth they built temples oriented
To favor stellar, solar and lunar alignments.

Oh, Temple of the Transparent Walls
And Golden Gates, speak to us!
Help us to understand ourselves
As Spiritual Beings! Can we not
Bind the sweet influences of the Pleiades,
Our "central sun" of religions, calendars, myths,
Tradition and symbolism and invite
Universal Love into our midst"?

Louise Horton
Granger, TX

LOVE POEM IN BLUE

i am all of you
take me.

i lie against you/an extended metaphore
in work shirt   between
blue black waves   of sheets.

sometimes we undulate
in these raw places
secret as snakes
our fox eyes beating in the luminous dark

but at the moment
we lie still
sated with our knowledge
breathing in the freshness
of new sheets
tailored and perfect
as soft flat leaves.

we speak
about the war
any war, our
frailities,
what you will do tomorrow
it makes no difference.

behind this language
tempered with need
and distance
this language of nouns
and future tenses

is the language
of our bodies
hung briefly here
and finally silent
a dark sacrifice
between wishes

a pulse/
of blood.

Noni Howard
Pacifica, CA

THE FLOWER MAN IN THE ALLEY

In space, nothing grows: a budding flower
floats timeless, the pain in parent and child,
the stinging waves of lost love and the hour
spent listening to direction. What wild
games we play, watching each other's strangled
expressions. Stars form familiar shapes,
almost fatherly images; the mangled
souls of space walkers, like myself, the rapes
of childhood freedom, the endless battle
to become, or not to become, Father,
all twisted into the outlined rattle
of his ghost. Why do I push him farther
away? All my life has been moon and star,
evenings left up to the sky. It is dark.

Eric Machan Howd
Slaterville Springs, NY

WHEN TRUE JOY IS TO GIVE

There is a chill to December
and a warmth to applaud;
above the glitter of brisk trade
the Christchild now is Lord.

And shops superfluous with food
will make our hands dig deep
in pockets, to supply the needs
of hungry folk who weep.

As this is a time for kindness
when true joy is to give
with generosity of heart
while we in plenty live.

The balm of gratitude and hope
as souls commune in peace;
shines with the tinsel on the tree
as love's wonders increase.

Christmas is for every man,
speaks to the humane cause;
recalls childhood and infancy
as smiling Angels pause,

To bless us in our jollity
and making light of things;
as the spirit from ages past
its Yuletide greeting brings.

Patricia Howe
England

EMIGRANTE

In the winter
the Castagnole* vineyards are dressed
                    in white coats
and dream of spring
                        rains

but you instead dreamt
                of America
like a moth pulled by a hundred watt bulb
until your wings

            grew stiff.

Elias N. Hruska
Los Gatos, CA

* Castagnole Monferrato
  Province of Piemonte
  Italy

WADINA FARM

Hunger rises, Fear
Hands clench tense around
I her trembling handles
She my quaking desire
Twisting, twisting
Further, further.
Muscles tense, the pace increasing
From low moans now screach
Thunderous roars
Terror screams
Until exhaustion comes
And both remain still
On their bed of damp grass.
Hunger rose; fear subsided
On Wadina Farm.

Steve Huck
San Francisco, CA

THE ARABIAN MOON

Glorious are the Arab Moon's flowing garments
Alabaster robes smoldering
Which undulate over powerful limbs and thighs.
You stride across heaven's deserts
Mounting the wildest of stars
A stallion of incomparable beauty.
Teeth flashing, sinews rippling
You charge the herd all a'tremble,
A dominating force, a clever rogue
Who influences and restrains
Your thrashing sea of mares.
Together you assault heaving continents far below.

The Arabian Moon's white hot eyes
Forged in the furnace of a universe
Command with laser scythe
A glistening stampede,
Foaming manes flying in a frenzy
To rein in and return, rein in and return.
They prance in quivering abandon
They neigh in manic joy,
Impudently tossing lovely proud heads
Adoring their protector and destiny.

How fair and how pleasant you are
Sharing delights oh my beloved.
The Arabian Moon cannot hold a candle to you.
Your influence holds the reins of my surging emotions.
The ebb and flow of my life
is controlled by your dominating force,
Commanding the glistening tides of my destiny.

Norma Hull
Vista, CA

A MOTHER WRITES TO HER PRIESTLY SON

Dear Father Rich.,

From heaven's realm, I write to you,
To thank you for your love and care,
The many acts of kindness, too,
And many hours you spent in pray'r.

You stood for hours from morn 'till night,
And saw how helpless there I lay.
You did not rest nor go away,
But tried to help in every way.

I saw the tears mount in your eyes.
Yet I pretended not to see.
I closed my eyes and prayed to God
To help you bear the hurt with me.

You have been faithful all your life,
You brought so much of joy and love,
My priestly son, now do not grieve,
I am so happy here above.

You see, it was when you left me,
That Jesus came to my sick bed.
He woke me up and took my hand,
"You're coming home with Me," He said.

And when He led me to the gates
Where Peter stood by with a key,
He flung the gates, they opened wide,
All Saints and Angels greeted me.

I cannot tell you what it's like
Where I have just begun to live.
In heaven, it's so beautiful,
Description of it, I can't give.

Let not your heart be heavy, son.
Do not be sad, shed not a tear.
Rejoice! Rejoice! And sing for joy,
I am so very happy here.

Mother

Sister Mary Kathryn Hyjek, O.S.F.
Omaha, NE

BEAUTY OF THE NIGHT

The sun has gone,
but not for long,
beauty of the night you are here.
Soft summer breeze,
with the fragrance of sweet gum trees,
and honey suckle vine.
Little fire fly,
as it blinks it's light in the clear night sky,
and the smell of fresh cut hay.
The bark of a dog,
as it finds a toad frog,
and sends it on its way.

Late night quiet,
the moon, the stars,
jupiter and mars,
and most of all the milky way.
Beauty of the night,
until first daylight,
and the beginning of a brand new day.

Weldon O. Isham
Mineral Wells, TX

LOVE IS...

a second language
in these hate-laced days.
Written in need and skin
it feeds on hunger
and wakefulness.

The mind cannot map
its syntax
nor figure out
the limits
of its ragged sentences.

When the heart sleeps,
this tongue
becomes silence
echoing
in drafty crevices
between dreams.

Louise Jaffe
Brooklyn, NY

DUSK REVEALED

The tiniest twigs
that lie flat against this orange sky
sing out their black clarity

and sink my breath

because—despite all
the black words I have put on paper—
I have still failed to explain myself.

Robert K. Johnson
Needham, MA

OUTSIDE SCHAGHTICOKE

Miles from civilization and certainty
And sure blue blood aristocracy
So far from crystal and porcelain
Fine lace, grace and satin

Thrust into a wilderness village
Thriving upon the land
Rustic settlers next to barbarian
Reveal simple kindness more genuine...

An heiress of considerable fortune
Who treasured since youth the strength of the quill
And comfort in a home on a hill
And culture in the meadows and streams

Now when distant thunders
Rattle the nearby mountainsides
Stands an orchard Orpheus in silhouette
On a hill behind the sun

Alonzo Augustus Jones
Tulsa, OK

JULY 4, 1776

Today, we salute the Signers
And the flag we love so dear,
Every day of our lives,
Not just once a year.

Today, we thank the Signers,
men of intelligence, courage and vision,
Who cut our ties with England,
making us free by their decision.

Today we bless the Signers,
And our gracious God above,
And freely give the United States
Our eternal love!

Alice Whiteside Jorg
Topeka, KS

BROWN LEATHER HANDS

the man with
leathery brown hands
ever so strong
on the handle
of a plow—
sun baked
tapestry face
sweat drenched brow
hard at work
sun up to
sun down
the man with
leathery brown hands
never dreaming of
places beyond,
content to follow
the furrow
tilling the land
honest and strong
as day is long,
the man with
leathery brown hands_____

Faye Kaestner
Louisville, KY

IN THE KITCHEN

your mission
grandma's chocolate chips.
whose succulent sweetness
seduced you to reach for more.
Hearing the clatter of
the cookie jar's cover
your brothers
rushed to protest
in raucous voice
how about leaving
some for us

now tears shed
(years too)
that sweet memory
is all
they have left
to savour.

Jean Kemper
East Hampton, NY

WHERE GOOD DOGS GO

As I stand beside her tiny grave
There's something that I know.
Though animals have no souls,
I know where the good dogs go.

She sleeps beneath a mound of dirt
Beside a tall Willow,
But this is not her final place
'Cause I know where the good dogs go.

There is a place within my heart
Where love is free to grow.
A place where memories never die,
A place where the good dogs go.

Loretta A. Kinley
Lafontaine, IN

COMPATRIOTS

My Mother's a "writer," a writer is she.
There's sugar in the stew and salt in the tea.
The washer is going with no clothes inside,
But Mother is happy creating a bride.
My Mother's a "poet," that's what she tells us.
She welcomes disorder with nary a fuss.
In all of our corners cobwebs may be seen,
But Mother's contented crating a queen.
My Mother's confusion means nothing to me.
I rather enjoy it for then I feel free
To work at some things that I think I can do,
While my Mother's composing *I'm* writing, too.

Betty Minor Kryah
Carrollton, OH

NORTH STAR

You call your mother's name,
ask for the love that once washed over you
like a warm bath.

You have fixed her in your firmament.
She is your North Star.

Toward what quadrant shall you steer
the fragile craft of your life,
life out of her fruiting body,

Her love was plucked too soon
before the fruit matured.

You look in a mirror rolling back years;
speak to a reflection, to a mother
wheeling a child across streets

trust in her innocent eyes,
looking to her North Star.

E. Landau
New York, NY

LADY OF THE LIGHTHOUSE

Come, let us trek to Monterey
    To watch the Lighthouse Ghost
She walks within the beacon's glow
    Above the rock strewn coast.

On moonless nights, she does appear
    Searching for her mate
She walks within the beacon's glow
    It's said this is her fate.

Betrayed her love, the story goes
    While he was far at sea
She walks within the beacon's glow
    In death she cannot flee.

Returning on the evening tide
    Dropped anchor in the bay
She walks within the beacon's glow
    In death she cannot stray.

Arriving home, an empty nest
    He vanished in the gloom
She walks within the beacon's glow
    Below, the breakers boom.

And now she walks in deep despair
    She'll never see dawn's light
She walks within the beacon's glow
    She's doomed to walk the night.

Raymond Le Rendu
Dallastown, PA

SUFFER

Suffering
Vinegar and Gall
The marinade of all resistance
Dabbed onto a cut become a gash
The stinging tincture makes it heal
As our teeth gnash
The pain is real that conditions existence

A tonic elixir distills in boiling to a roll
A formula fulfills that nourishes the soul
The acid makes the ego burn
Excoriates old patterns
Change exacts its toll
Enables nothing but the will to learn...
A burden lifts, a cycle turns

The crucible, the cauldron, the urn
In every sentient vessel
She pours it on with love
Bliss' antithesis cascades from above
Oppressive in our midst
Invades from below...
A catalyst for death unless we grow

Leslie Levy
Los Angeles, CA

WORKING HAND IN HAND

The soul and the body
Disputing one day;
And this to the body
I heard the soul say,
"Come back to your senses
You're going astray.
And if you're not careful
With my life you'll pay."

The soul did persuade him
With this narrative,
So, off he did go for
Applied sedative;
For sound was the treatment
The doctor did give,
For in curing the body
The soul will outlive.

Sister Virginia Liberatore, MPF
Morristown, NJ

THE DREAM OF LIFE I ONCE WAS
("Goodbye drunken ghost." Allen Ginsberg's
        final words to Jack Kerouac)

One Ohio morning, I awoke
To a dream of life
that had its murky beginnings
Long before I was born.

Distant, far beyond what I could
Fully recall, were old
Friends. Friendships I had
Nurtured like small lambs
With the milk of my childhood.

Somehow my dream my life,
Moved and exploded into thousands
Of different philosophies, directions and ideas.
Somehow, I became
Tangled in the webs of my memories
And I lost the grip on my old friends'
Hands. Friendships I had force
Weaned, but I did more. I did
Worse. I forgot
Them. I left
Them. I never returned
Until I was too far out
Beyond, and too late to return
To those days of innocent
Child's play. But I have
Grown just enough
To hear the bellowing
From my ghost friends' whispers,
Their very faint voices tell
Me to put my ear against
The giant seashell of any neighbor's backyard
And to listen to the sea of myself
Rolling and wailing. Their voices,
In and Out, moving and pumping
The aging blood in my heart.

M. L. Liebler
St. Clair Shores, MI

THE NEIGHBORHOOD

The neighborhood is changing, she said
taking about her neighborhood

which was, even though she still lived there

(but perhaps didn't want to)

becoming someone else's neighborhood
which would make it a strange neighborhood

(at least for her
even though she still lived there)

and changed from the old neighborhood
which was a good neighborhood

so that although it was still an old neighborhood
it was no longer the good old neighborhood

that it was before the strangers

(even though they also became neighbors
or would have become neighbors if they could)

came

and, of course, because strangers make everything strange
and also make everything change

the old neighborhood, which still was
in a strange way, her neighborhood

was no longer a good neighborhood

(even though the neighbors might have been good
or would have been good if things had been different

and they weren't so strange)

and it was even worse than living
in a bad neighborhood

(which all neighborhoods were becoming)
because there was no place for anyone to go

because all the neighborhoods
already had new neighbors and new strangers

and were changing...

Leatrice Lifshitz
Pomona, NY

THE FUNNEL

The sifting sands flow quickly in the spout.
They shift and slide, come pouring out.
Into something larger, or into
something better, more
suited to holding
these sands of
time. A holder
for these
sands
of
m
i
n
e

Tom Lin
Miami, FL

CREVE COEUR

Heart disease, the doctor said.
But not cigarettes nor cream tarts
felled milady.
Rather, the battery of careless speech
and thoughtless acts
bruised her tattered heart.
Till premature grief
rent the keloid maze.

Carol Jean Locke
Manassas, VA

THE FARMER'S HORSES

He was young on a farm,
Where spring was open-handed fragrance.
In the halo of dawn, he harnessed Annie and Chester
And let them drink from the singing brook,
Before ploughing the rich loam in butter-soft furrows.
Summer was hot corn fields, and blossoms bent by bees;
Fall was apples gathered and a barn full of hay.
Then, life was so shining and simple
Like supper at end of the day.

All his journeying after those good days,
Disappeared in a blur of galloping time.
There were corridors of cities, rows of fences,
Rooms with small pillows of comfort.
The clocks in his mind stopped somewhere.
Like aging stones, years crumbled and fell around him.
Once there was happiness and love;
But gone, all gone - lost in the underbrush.
Only Annie and Chester kissed his frosty glove.

Then came the nursing home,
With nudges of memories churning his mind,
Like crashing storms and unreasonable arguments.
He called Annie and Chester all night long.
The people complained, He disturbed them.
They wanted to know who Annie and Chester were.
While they meant to be kind,
He should be taken away.
In his state, he really couldn't mind.

But the farmer held onto his invisible reins.
The horses hooves were easy in winter wheat.
Sometimes he let them run free in the gladness of grass.
The night he died, he didn't call them;
But that was because Annie and Chester were there,
Breathing in the darkness, quenching hunger, drinking water,
Standing warm beside him, heads bent, intimate they knew,
That no man lives forever—but sometimes horses do.

Florence Lonsford
New York, NY

WISDOM SMILING

An oracle hissed: The best thing is not
To be born; the second, to be buried young.
Uncompromising Nietzsche retorted: Dung!
Although living is painful, why rot
In agony? Turn to laughter, sublime
Prerogative of gods and men. "Goldy,"*
Earlier, employed laughing comedy,
Unmasking genteel, sentimental mime.
Today, despite corruption, crime, and drugs,
The sanity of gaiety prevails.
Ignore decibelated doomsday wails
Of profit-seeking prophets, propped on rugs—
Unclean, unkempt, wearing outlandish garb;
Lilting laughter's wiser than a slob's sob.

Richard L. Loughlin
Kew Gardens, NY

THE WAY OF THE WIND

In early spring the warm winds
blow
to whisk away late flakes of
snow,
out of the ever changing
sky
the sightless currents swiftly
fly.
When summer comes the warming
gale
shoots new leaves where others
fell,
high above gentle clouds float
by
while nesting songbirds sing and
sigh,
The green of summer soon turns
brown
and leaves of autumn seek the
ground,
colors of fall high ride the
breeze
until at last stand leafless
trees.
Winter's tempest comes with a
rush
followed by a cold gloomy
hush,
each year the pattern will
begin
for so it is...the way of the
wind.

M. Rosser Lunsford
Eatonton, GA

TIES

The smile, the eyes—a handsome man.
Above her dresser, Sister keeps
this wedding picture of you, Dad.
Except for it, we'd never seen
you in a white bow tie and tux.

Sister chose not to marry.
Your disapproval of the man
I wanted for my first made you
refuse to walk me down the aisle.
Mother had to take your place.

After the rites, I learned your clear
deep eyes had slipped into the back
of the church. Somehow you knew
the marriage would not last. At my
informal second, only preacher,
two witnesses, bride and groom.

You knew this knot would bind a quarter
of the century, knit four children.
Knew that it would link me still
though the legal bond untied
sixteen years ago.

        You've been
dead fifteen of them. Now wear
your tux and tie, Daddy, to walk
me down the last of life's long aisle.

Annette Lynch
South Pasadena, CA

LEDA AS AN OLD WOMAN

No one remembers any more
how I flew through stars
to find my name, carried

the basket with seven stones
until each turned to pure crystal.
The swan was nothing, you

understand—a jab and thrust
quickly dismissed, black feathers
loose on the ground—no matter

he called himself Thunder Strikes,
air hissing in his beak.
What I mean is the way

gold flowered in me, all
my shadows dancing wild
as one, two, three, four

mouths and hearts took shape
to give me wings. *Free:*
how many women ever know

full bend and stretch of that
blue word? My children brought me
sky, a deathless journey past

their own destruction (even bitter
tears subside) and made me Queen
Forever of all colors, all light.

Katharyn Howd Machan
Ithaca, NY

JOURNEY

This island keeps scooting further
and further out to sea asleep
in waters deep as ignorance.

Along the wallpaper horizon,
no Coast Guard cutter sights survivors,
no luxury liners slice

into the solid sprawl of ocean,
We look for oars with teeth of steel
to propel us back to shore

or magnets with lure enough
to convince the metals of hard-packed soil
they are stronger than wayward stars.

As cross winds buffet,
where we are depends on the view.
The island waffles, cools its roots

in byways that slip in and out
of context in search of a mariner,
a gust of air to raise the roof

to the open blue, above waters
familiar enough to trust, to rock
us back to the birthday cake in the kitchen,

no longer a wedge broken off
set loose to bobble
witlessly without compass

on a journey begun long ago.

Leona Mahler-Sussman
Cedar Grove, NJ

O LOVE

O cherished One, how can I tell
Of fairer grace than I believed could be;
Of sweetness, fuller than a nectared swell
Of flowered air, come of you to me.

Beloved One, the softest inner fire
Glows heart-deep in your faintest sigh,
And through love's affinity of desire
Ignites my heart, as we are coming nigh.

O one alone, I would not know another,
Enough that life and love remain this flame;
O let our yearnings yield and burn together—
Love always different, always yet the same.

John Manier
Dayton, OH

I MISS YOU

Sometimes
I see you
and an
occasional nod
or smile
will do.
But nights like tonight
I need more.
I miss the talks
we shared,
the walks
we took,
and the hugs
you gave.
These little bits
of comfort
and friendship
are treasured
and I miss them.
I miss you.

Amanda Marbach
Converse, TX

THE LANGUAGES OF THE FLOWERS

They speak for themselves
They speak to us, for us
saying what we are dumb before
these Messengers of Beauty.

Species speak in dialects
of colors, shapes, forms, scents.
And enlightened or knowing ladies & gents
"buy" Thee symbols free in blooms so heaven-scent.

Symbols saying specifics as so assigned
by human beings to Lives Divine
expressing through the flower-lore
—carnations, roses as from days of yore.

But, can symbols be as pure or as refined
as full efflorescence undefined
when we feel Thee Glory
of such Divine Designs?

Fred Marchman
Mobile, AL

BENEATH THE HALO

Divine and undefiled,
  her beauty unexcelled
The magic of her smile
  initiates the spell.

She recites the incantation
  with a whisper from her lips.
The wind blows thru the nations
  and into each ear slips.

Safe beneath the halo,
  untouched, she touches all.
The colours of the rainbow
  are at her beck and call.

Eternally maternal,
  her garden flowers bloom
With a radiance supernal
  and a scent of fine perfume.

She wears the robe of seasons
  that in a circle dance.
She has and keeps her reasons
  for leaving naught to chance.

A. V. Santa Maria
Rahway, NJ

POOR ALEX

Afflicted from his mother's loss, he cried
And felt the dark hour of his destiny;
His last gaze fell on Wied-il-Ghajn and sighed,
Following then the kind call of clemency.

There he found young sweet Rose of his same age
Who quickly taught him how to read and write!
He was glad in his master's patronage
And loved immensely Rose with all his might.

Mountainous black clouds formed again for him,
He fought with some school boys defending Rose
And suffered from a bad maid's Gossiping.
When Rose left to nuns' schooling, he missed a rose.

Alex handled well his master's boat,
But died when angry sea his body smote.

Victor Marroun
Zejtun - Malta

MAN SHOT IN ROSE GARDEN
"We called for backup, but by then they had trouble understanding
us. We were calling for Jesus, too."

Buffalo Police Officer, as quoted in
Buffalo News

Dear granddaughters.
Here is the snapshot you took of me
in your Uncle Jim's archetypal garden.

I am seventy-five here,
and lately, in whatever garden
wonder if it will be my last....

Not to worry.
Fresh out of apples, anyway.
So why should I stroke from shadowed sleep
any serpents I might meet?

Grown
you'll understand this poem.
I hope (for you who also write
and paint) readers, and lookers
who won't need words like "archetypal."

You'll write better poems than I do
about gardens, and apples
...and even snakes.

Never did get the hang of it.
Never could use one word where two would do.
Or choose the short one over
the long.

Always wanted to show off my vocab
and not, like Jesus, merely
doodle in the sand just 'cause some guy
threw stones at some dame who was wearing
the wrong kind of clothes
and was probably "asking for it," anyway.

But even the cops, now, are
calling for
Jesus.

Read Frost, and take the road
less traveled.
It's safer.

Love: Your grandmother.

Grace B. Martin
Buffalo, NY

GHOST OF REFLECTION

I am as old
as the stars in the dark sky
shining in all the rooms
of the world.

I was created by
all the hate of the world
so I could make everyone
love everything.

To tell you how I look
is hard
because how I look
in my eyes
is not how I look
in someone else's.

I sound like the voice
in the mind that tells
right from wrong.

I live only in the mind
when summoned.
When not summoned
I live in the gorgeous blue sky.

I drink the love and eat
away the hate.

My powers are the unthinkable,
I can do anything
and more.

I do not know how people think of me
for I am not them.

I cannot say what my future will bring
for God himself does not know.

Kami Lee Martin
Elkhart, IN

FROM SLUMBER

Face in a dream, your hand took my hand,
reached from the dream to lead me away—
to see how holy is each grain of sand
take it again and let us away away.
Fearful perhaps, perhaps fearing to know
how small is my dream that I would not go.
Yet — tarry awhile to give me time
to leave fears for my narrow dream behind
because I know there is so much to know,
so much to learn. Face in my dream
guide me to wonder at what my dream hides.
Take my hand; help me rise from slumber.
I don't want to sleep this lifetime away;
away, asleep, of so much unconscious,
of days passing by, days without number.
In eternal perspective, each lifetime
is as the flick of a finger,
the blink of an eye.
But for me on this earth still,
still in deep dreaming slumber,
tomorrow, who knows? Today well and alive,
I urge you to help me! I want to be wakened.
Take my hand. Hold it tight! Be my guide.
Sigh for me gently while I hesitating,
while fearful of leaving am eager to go
for, attached to this lifetime
and the dream I am living, I ask:
Do I want to wake from my dreaming slumber,
aware of those lifetimes that I let slip by?
From deep slumber to consciousness waking,
aware of life more than the blink of an eye,
face in my dream, perhaps from lifetimes
past making; both dreamer and dream,
take my hand. Let us fly!

Vivian L. Martinetz
El Paso, TX

BITTERSWEET

Finger paint.
Splashed bright
Against the
Untouched page of sky...

Autumn trees,
Entwined and oranged
With cascading bittersweet,
Fling one final
Wordless boast
'Til they undress,
And, stripped complete,
Lay down their
Tattered robes of color—
A cushion for His feet.

...A spectrum which
Bestirs such envy
That the sunset
Holds its breath,

While the
Bittersweet sings
Of mystery,
Sings of
The life of death.

Sister Joseph of Jesus, Mary, OCD
Terre Haute, IN

BOUNTIFUL ONCE MORE

Emerging slowly from her gilded walls,
she left behind the long-accustomed glitter
to free herself from all-intrusive clutter,
to grope her way back into higher halls.
She turned her mind toward the neglected ills
of those least privileged, their lives a litter
of listlessness, existing behind a shutter
of alienation, addicts cursed by pills.

Rejected first, a Lady Bountiful
seeming to play this charitable act
she shed her fancy speech along with dress
of showy cloth. No longer in the role
of temporary help, she added grace and tact
toward giving of herself with new noblesse.

Anne Marx
Hartsdale, NY

BILLET DOUX

Only *2* letters 'twixt love and lose
one is *T* and the other is *U*
Go back to *A* go home and *B*
Come out and play
Come back to me

It's *E* it's *F* ed it's *G*
it's *H* i   I wish I was
I fell in the *O* of O's
I felt the woe because
I felt your claws

it's *C*   It's shell and it's shaking
it's hot   It's *H* ell and it's aching
tell me *Y* I still feel proprietary
When it's so inappropo

Marcia K. Matthews
Belmont, MA

CONSIDER IT OUR SURVIVAL KIT

Sunset: my muse

    With its soft pinks and purples
    touching the horizon
    I wistfully look at you and smile
    (You're the night-owl)

Dawn: your mistress

    With its dusty blues and dappled-grays
    A gentle, calm, patient soul
    You playfully look at me and wink
    (I'm the early-bird)

By writing,
knowledge of life follows—
I will create child-like magic
You will erase adult-ridden lies.

We work, play and live hard lives these days
Our imagination must continue...

consider it our survival kit.

Maria Jan Matula
La Mesa, CA

FORT FUNSTON* AT SUNSET

That bluff, earth's coastal assertion high above
the turbulent, insistent Pacific, where men
come to try their angel wings, hang
gliding like Icarus toward the for—
ever slipping away, blushing sun:
this is where a select city stops,
where America ends, where lost dreams
thrash like the surf below and rise up,
reborn in the hair-whipping, echoic, salt—
bitten winds that sting with esoteric secrets.

You are disoriented. Here, far beyond America's
righteous right-wingers, the heartless limits
of human love, the fear that locks doors,
erects forts, your soul lifts up,
buoyed by the incantations of
Land's End* wind and waves, and
soars over dunes held in place by clumps
of ash green, succulent ice plants sprouting
their pink and white stars. For once, then, just
before blood-vermillion light explodes toward China,

    you discover your wings, blue as a timid breeze,
green as the surge of the sea,
    frail as flesh-webs in day's final firelight.

Thomas R. McKague
Tully Lake, NY

*Golden Gate National Recreation Area, San Francisco

LANDMARKS IN THE HEART

Her house that harboured carousels of song,
Where love sprang up and blossomed all year long,
Whose walls enclosed the goldenness of laughter
That built life's blessings into every rafter;
Where death and sorrow took their somber part,
Yet caring comforted the heavy heart—
So much of life bound up in brick and stone—
And now that brick and stone completely gone!

Landmarks succumb to grading blade and plow—
Only the landmarks in our hearts stand now.
Only the precious wording of her verse will be
markers of where her spirit here made melody.

Kathryn Evans McKay
Walton, KY

WOOD WORDS -REFLECTION

I dwelt awhile amidst the trees
And longed for peace
I felt it in the gentle breeze
That gave my cares release

I watched the stately pines ascend
And asked for strength
It issued from the roots below
Which gave the trees their length

I listened to the rustle of the leaves
And asked to know the way
Life is a response, they said
The 'yes' of every day

I watched the sun shine through the woods
And asked for light
I found it in the colors and the hues
That danced within my sight

I listened to the singing of the birds
And asked for joy
I found it in my every prayer
And in the Lord's reply

I left the woods and went my way
To meet with humankind
I now had strength and joy and peace
And light to guide and find.

Sister Teresa McMahon, SSL
Long Beach, CA

TO A GRANDCHILD

I watch you as you sleep here in my arms
Your silken lashes resting on your cheeks
Your elfin mouth curled up into a tiny bow
Where every now and then, a smile creeps

Dream on, dear little One, your lovely dreams
While those of us who hold you watch and smile
And pray for the young man that you'll become some day
But, stay a precious baby for a while

Just let us clasp your chubby, dimpled hand
And guide your faltering steps as first you try
To walk alone, declare your independence
Yes, let us hold you tightly e'er you fly

Then, fill our days with sunshine with your twinkling smile
As you raise your arms up for a hug and kiss
And let us hope, if only for a little while
That life will stay as simple as all this

For dearest Child, you've won us, each and every heart
And in our worlds, you have a special place
For all our days become a little brighter
Each time we see your dimpled, smiling face

Marian Grady McNeely
Palatine, IL

BLUE YOUR EYES

this edge of snow
in silent sky.
Brown eyes soft
tree bark patterns as
yellow flicks
sparkle in wintry sun.

And now it seems
your eyes are green
green as spruce
turning to grey eyes
glancing across as if
from a mountainside.

Your eyes two violets
hidden beneath frost.
Close your eyes
as sleepless stars
glide through night
in aerial ballet.

Black coal eyes
glowing on fire
red flames leaping
out of eyes burning
blue your eyes.

Joan McNerney
Brooklyn, NY

SUPERLATIVE

O sun of sky so warm and bright
Earth cannot live without your light.

Yet, sweet smile so sublime
You are more precious to mankind.

But You o Son of Light and Love
Are the most treasured Gift from God above.

Helen M. McPhillips
Windham, NH

DRIFTING

Days flow by like
tiny streams merging
into a river of memories.

Memories flow gently
upon demand, and quietly
the streams and river unite.

Tendrils of lingering dreams,
hanging like Spanish moss across the mind's
eye, gently drift along birthing a memory.

Misty dreams materialize and grow in form.
The stream of consciousness carries them
along.

One day the dreams crystalize,
the streams form a body,
the river grows strong,
and the mind lives again.

Keith McUmber
Minneapolis, MN

BABY SHOWER
At the Laura Russo Gallery

Streetlights come on but it is
The museum that darkens

I look through plate glass
Into the mouth of its cave

Bright canvas fused glass fade
The art I see is the circle

Of chairs ribbons on the floor
Women eating strawberries

Spreading brie on sliced baguette
I love the one past eighty

Who seems sculptured on a folding
Metal chair draped in a long

Tartan skirt red blouse she
Rises from the unwrappings

At this opening of the unborn
Among so much knitting so much

Unraveling as I see it all
Bison grazing on rock wall

Antelope leaping over the arch
Woodcut salmon spawning

A school of fossiled prints
Onto the sidewalk

Where I make sentinel
And listen for drums

Phil Meehan
Portland, OR

TOLSTOY AT YASNAYA POLYANA

He wanted to be like Jesus
but he was rich, and married besides—

impediments to sainthood, or even
telling the truth. Still, he was a genius

whose vision would have been just as just
if written in a peasant's smoky hut

instead of Yasnaya, which he loved
for its fields and feathery birch flush

against that house still standing sturdier
than Russia. Yasnaya Polyana molded him as much

as London made Dickens—imagine him at dusk
by the cold lake imagining old Bolkonsky

with his wig: *'And why should she marry?' he thought*—
moving toward the quivering page, and us!

Peter Meinke
St. Petersburg, FL

WAVES
(In memory of Barbara)

Our lives are like the ocean waves coming ashore.
Sand, shells and pebbles wash in the wake.
The tide goes out leaving its mark.

And so with people, we also come ashore
    making our mark.
The tide leaves and we drift into eternity.

Refreshment of the waves focuses in our
    memories giving us strength.

Lorraine Melanson
Hawthorne, NJ

QUERY

The bite of Cleo's snake would strike as deep
In any other breast.
Tears shed for her
Were not more copious or sad
Than those choked out
Above a nameless serving girl's,
Not noted then and scarce remembered now.

Turn back in time and look upon the both.
If someone should remove the crown of gold,
The golden bier
Could you then say who was more greatly mourned?
Who was more dear?

Ruth de Menezes
Santa Monica, CA

TOO FREQUENT MOURNINGS

Death news of dear ones
shoots slivers in the heart
torn from weathered boards
of recollection. But fast pace
will not allow slow dirge and wail.
Swift accolade memorial
dismisses pathos—
whisks us to stifling work domain
bristled with remembrance
that wears heart tissues thin.
No brush off! Another death word stabs,
and then another. More and more
our requiems engulf the self until
Donne's "ask not for whom the bell tolls,
it tolls for thee" bangs us to acquiescence.

Eleanora Miller
Leon, IA

A MATTER OF WHEN

I took a quiet walk today
Inside my restless mind
Searching for those long lost
    thoughts
That loneliness seems to find.—
'Till snuggling there in a
    vapor
Just beyond my touch
There purred a pretty kitten
I used to love so much.
I remember trying to save him
That day out in the street
But now I take a quiet walk
And in my mind we meet.

M. Chvat Minot
Pacific Palisades, CA

HEARTSTRINGS

What are they, these heartstrings
Are they something important
Are they something real
    Can one see them with the naked eye
    Can one pluck them as a note on the harp
    Are they necessary to living?

A part of daily life
Their nature, though not physical,
Is something one can feel
    Not observed with the human eye
No one can flick a finger
    And twang a note or two
But rather, one perceives
    The strength and laxing of
    Such invisible chords
    Which gently flow between loved ones.
Their number is limitless
Just enough to touch with outstretched hand
    Or miles away, far from sight.

There comes a tug when the lines get taut
When one is aware of the expanding flow—
    A radiation of power
    Which travels across time and space
    To someone of meaning.

Frazzled and frayed in rare moments
    When misunderstanding arises
But elastic enough to spring back
    Again and again
To continue stretching and reaching
To be in touch with someone out there.

E. L. Moore
Medford, NJ

JUNGLE CREED

Survival of the fittest is a creed
The jungle made in days of grave distress
When beast ate beast for food, no more or less
Than really served the vast and desperate need;
But man from such demands and shackles freed
Should show a kind regard and gentleness
For those of lesser strength. All true success
Is best displayed within the noble deed.

All real enduring greatness lies in this,
In being kind to beast and fellow-man,
In humbly serving truth as best one can...
In reaping from that service all the bliss
That peace can give the world without a flaw
When ruled by love that ends the jungle law.

Goldie L. Morales
Monterey Park, CA

IN LUNDQUIST PARK GOD'S ORDER RULES

Seeds float in the air, lazy as a daisy.
White tufts drift along; if weather were colder, hazy,
seeds could be mistaken for snow if seen
from a distance. Seeds in reams
make the hour seem dreamy.

Squirrels chase after one another, limber.
They're sporting as they climb up timber.
Birds pierce air with their loud sweet cries.
Through the pine trees breezes sigh.
Over it all the sky's so high.

The fat muskrat scurries under the bridge
when it spies me for I'm no midget.
The spring season rapidly wanes into summer
as a bumblebee almost grazes my nose
when soon there will be roses.

Park attendants water flowers, use special tanks.
The gladiolus are standing in ranks.
Their blossoms are being withered by time
as I walk through the Park, no dimes for my rhymes
and feel anything but stymied.

Barbara Mosemann
Wakarusa, IN

LITTLE PATH

Mysterious path, where do you lead?
Perhaps to the heights where little
        lambs feed.
The Good Shepherd, did He at times
        pass this way
When He went alone to our Father to
        pray?
When He called His sheep did His voice
        resound?
Ah! truly blest, tis' holy ground.

Sister Mary of the Nativity, OP
West Springfield, MA

UPPER ECHELON

The eyes that saw you walking
only yesterday have
undergone retreat and
readjusted vision for today

To my amazement, blue is really red
and red is blue - and
I need time for reevaluation
of myself and you

The road to selfless love
is cumbersome and far
I'm not quite ready to admit
how tall you really are

Ruth M. Nebbie
Port Orange, FL

$C_{27}H_{45}OH$

Learning the formula won't disarm the things
that float in your blood or dispel the gang
of mavens around your heart. No luck:

this witchcraft's been with you since birth.
It is the scarab lodged lower than your throat,
a Milky Way nebulous, close and enraged.

You wonder if there could be a miracle
to hang on your walls. Would it be
apocryphal from the start: the phony

hope, the dream that cures the body? Yours
is a foreign faith learned without gurus,
for you know, yes, you know it is your poem:

the rhymes and cadences written for you.
An exhalation: the old synonym for life.

Judith Neeld
Menemsha, MA

MOTHER NIGHT

The arrows of the west wind,
   The javelins of the sun
Are spent; night, the huge night
   With a whisper has begun
To cradle in her arms all things
   Grown weary, every one,
Lulled as the birds of folded wings,
   Lulled as the day that is done,
As the arrows of the west wind,
   The javelins of the sun.

Richard Nickson
New York, NY

SECOND AVENUE SENRYU SEQUENCE

> tricycle race —
> moving van swerves
> in the nick of time
>
> teenage blonde
> with a strawberry cone
> nurses her baby
>
> sale sensation —
> buy one wheelchair
> get another free
>
> outside the shop
> locksmith reading comics
> in his swimsuit
>
> museum bench —
> girl in a neckbrace peers
> at the stock market news
>
> lunch break —
> interracial shootout
> with water pistols

H. F. Noyes
Greece

WISDOM FROM THE ENEMY

We are in your banks ....
We are in your police force ...
We, the Enemy,
Aim to subjugate your land ...
We are merciless brigands ...

Indeed, tomorrow
Sorrow will scourge you all day ...
Unless you all pray ...
Unless you all focus on
The Black madonna and Child ...

Martin J. O'Malley, Jr.
Passaic, NJ

THE LORD IS MY TEACHER

The Lord is my teacher; I am constantly learning.
Just when I think I have mastered life's lessons, Plop!
I fall flat on my face.
But from my gentle teacher, I learn how to get up again.
Yes, I begin anew with a lot more trust this time.
Some lessons are sheer delight!
They are learned from people He allows to enter my life.
He is so alive in them!
When I count on them too much though, or want to possess them, they
    disappear.
After grieving because of this loss, I find myself more attached to this
    teacher of mine.
He is becoming my security.
Sometimes I am allowed glimpses of my Teacher's glory, and I become
    ecstatic.
These times don't last too long, but they are filled with high
    voltage energy.
So I keep returning for new information; His lessons never disappoint me.
Messages are often the same, yet He shows me a new enticing way to view
    them.
This method engraves His words and actions more deeply on my heart.
It never ceases to amaze that when I am running on empty, He fills
    me to overflowing.
I don't like being emptied though, so I often make this lesson more
    difficult for my teacher.
Even though I am stubborn and reluctant, my teacher understands.
How well He knows that I am not ready, or refuse to be, so He patiently
    waits.
And when I am ready, the sheer joy of knowing that I am loved and
    teachable is mine.
With overflowing gratitude I continue my life's journey.
I wait and long for the day when I freely run into my Teacher's arms.
My lessons will be over and together we will savor our experiences.
O what JOY, GLORY, AND DELIGHT will be mine!
I will have become ONE with this compassionate teacher of mine!

Sister Mary Rita Omlor, O.S.F./T
New Washington, OH

MAKING UP MOTHER

I have always needed her
slender, tall with a nose that looks
good in profile. I would give her
an upsweep, shaven legs, high heels,
seamless nylons. She would never
make her own aprons. Dressed in
store-bought prints, she would laugh
until she cried.

Now mute, she can only point and nod,
make sounds that range through fury
or joy, a persistent keening. I offer
lipstick and powder, the Cara Nome
I remember, its beige dust in a box.
She always liked moody colors,
bruises on her mouth and cheekbones.

I find her lipstick, scrub plum
on the hollows of her face, give her
a mask of Dusty Rose. Her lips resist
a stiff line, slack since the stroke,
manage a fragile pucker where I dab
fuchsia. It slides to her front teeth,
stains the dentures as it has always.

Today, pleased with her face, the one given
to me, Mom asks me with a gesture
that I pull the stray hairs on her upper lip.
Age hairs of dark skins—I, too, have them.
They drag us down, unsightly wires of common
blood, that inextricable tangle.

Verlena Orr
Portland, OR

SOBBINGS

The sunlight's golden sobbing
that works itself out as rain
the twilight's grayish settling downpour
and the rains of the century

As you look into the goblet
of the moon's silver outpourings
you tell yourself something's shiny
but is it for you?

As the moonlit hills
surrender their bluish glint
do you sometimes wonder
if the tint was for your eyes alone?

And, in midnight's graceful surrender,
does the artist feel lesser
for the grandeur of the purple—
heeled moment of grace?

Susan Osterman
New York, NY

SOUNDS

These sounds I've learned to for them care,
As they make passage through the air.
The sound of ocean wind through screen,
Plus banshee's call in its eaves scream.
Hot whirl wind's passage through the corn,
Where fam'ly lived on our old farm.
The hen's brag cackle around noon,
When she left nest another boon.
The rooster's crow in the twilight,
While fam'ly prepared for the night.
The echo of a running train,
The fall on tin roof of a rain.
The creak of saddle as we rode,
And creak of harness as team strove,
To turn a furrow of black ground,
While odor of fresh earth sent 'round.
The caw of raucous crow in field,
While wood pecker makes dead wood yield.
Wind flapping sheets is now sound old,
Mom who washed them, in good sheep fold.
Their sound replaced by flag on pole.
Flag's battle with the wind is bold.
Friend had a camp where red birds sang.
Long gone the friend and his camp land.
In turn we had our camp site too,
Where rain frogs would their calls issue.
The waves would lap upon the shore,
But we no longer hear their roar.
In my back yard I am confined,
To dream of sounds of other times.
Soft falls the rain as if to weep,
To try with me old sounds to keep.

Donald Owen
Hallettsville, TX

NEW YEAR'S EVE

The old year did not attempt
to slink away unnoticed,
worn out and weary,
shackled to discarded dreams
and hopes unfulfilled,
fettered to feelings
of despair.

Unexpectedly a blue moon climbed
slowly in the eastern sky.
It lay above the river's water
like a blue and pink balloon,
tethered with a slender string
of reflected points of light,
inviting us to reach for it
and celebrate.

Mary Overfield
Henderson, KY

TEARS FROM HEAVEN

As I walked out in the
open, the breeze began to sway.
Then walked up to my treehouse
where I went up to pray.

I sat then in it's shelter
just me and the sky above.
Then I looked up to the
heavens for all the ones
I love.

I closed my eyes for once,
to remember past times ago.
Then started to see rain
drops, falling very slow.

I opened my eyes and
noticed, It was not from
God's own sky. They were
tears of love for others
who's love had made me cry.

Melissa Padilla
Uvalde, TX

ARCHES NATIONAL PARK

Blazing red stone
baked in the Utah sun.
Little by little erosion
forms a window for the sky.

Strange that
in its diminishment
is its beauty.

Bernadette Palma
Milwaukee, WI

MAKE IT EXTRAORDINARY

second by second,
minute by minute,
hour by hour,
the years pass by,
before you know it,
the new year becomes old,
the children grow older,
and the newborn baby's in preschool,
today, your first day with the company,
tomorrow, you retire, to collect pension,

the years pass us by,
don't become trapped in the "good ole days,"
live in the present, not past or future,
make these the "good ole days,"

Hold onto those years of youth,
but not for dear life,
because they'll pass you by,
live each second to the fullest,
old words, but oh so true,
One day we all turn around,
to find life's just spinning us round,
and we wonder what happened to those ten years,
they've slipped down the drain,
never to return,

My message,
make your short life extraordinary,
because when you blink,
your eyes never reopen.

Dennis Paul
Masury, OH

SONG OF THE SEA

The ships are whisked with the sea,
cresting on hell's rain,
wounds that open into each other,
the last blood burst of sky,
where all the clouds are nameless,
building seams underneath the air.

Here are the ragged crags, the
majestic juts of the sea lying just
beneath the parting waters, the
beach drenched with dusk, the
elegant night swimming in on white
waves, the sky open with motion.

Before the brush of horizons, a
step of silence flashes on stone,
a lost ship on the bottom of the
ocean with its doors open, waiting for
whatever comes into its domain, the
pull of treasures, men coming up mad.

Gulls mark the sea with shouts. Shadows
of wings shreading the sky, full of beasts.
Fish leaping and singing at the horizon
where the sun burns o range, siloueting herons
in flight. The stars breaking through at
dusk, dissolving the day with stardust.

Mario A. Petaccia
Tallahassee, FL

WELL-LOVED
(Sacred Heart 1993)

I took you to each
well-loved place because
you are well-loved:

Brown-bag breakfast above
the bay, and when we sat
down to eat our Irish oatmeal,
the hay was so high and heady
we could not see the water.
But, oh, the vulnerable vista
you opened to me amidst
the quaking grass.

A miniature beach crammed with
driftwood, exquisite contours,
leaning against your thigh,
book-bearer as you read a
Celtic romance complete with
ancient monastic site and
Scotch broom in the crevices.

The greenhouse a cozy
refuge from the May
rain hard and musical—
torrent of grace, redemptive
conspiracy — I will walk with
you around the distant bend
however long it takes.

M. Dilecta Planansky, O.S.B.
Shaw Island, WA

FRUSTRATING CATCH

A fisherman cast his bait
and he caught
first a Jew
then a Christian
then a Catholic
then a Protestant
and so forth.

Finally he exclaimed.
"What the devil!
Not one fish in the entire sea
a man could eat!"

Mariquita Platov
Tannersville, NY

WINTER LANDSCAPED

Giant paint brushes silhouetted
    against the winter sky;
Snow falls, softly and gently, and
    soon dark bark and branches are
    dressed in white fur.
Occasional creaks and groans punctuate
    the silence;
Hems and haws in the stillness of
    the night
Speak of God and Creation, and
    Of Life and Death.

Mary L. Plowe
Cincinnati, OH

A CAMPER'S SEASON

There are so few in our allotted years.
Will this time finally hold enough
of hours drawn out forever warm,
intensely warm upon the limbs,
while insects murmur on the ears?

And will there be enough cool streams—
gentler now than in spring's rush—
inviting waders farther out,
to play, refreshed from midday drowse?

Enough of reddened berries
tempting dusty hikers
to stop and savor
rolling ripened, rain-washed morsels
on the tongue?

Enough of days in sheltering giants—
touching with hungry fingertips
the damp sponginess of moss,
the dry rigidness of bark—
enough calm days to worship skyward
through spires of pine and fir?

How many nights to lie in forest duff,
know earth through the inmost bones,
brief moments shed our finite selves
to join another galaxy
as we reach toward stars
and drift asleep?

Judith Ahrens Powell
Richland, WA

LEGACY

She enters my home,
my heart. Her eyes sift
confusion. People & places
mock her now, enticing sighs
from ancient ghosts of
friends, & lovers who
betrayed her. Her children,
one confident, one shy, one capricious,
now meld into faint memories.

As she departs, her step
quickens in rhythm to a tune
no one can hear. I move
with her, wrap myself
in her mother-arms. Time
& tide will pass us by,
& ancient ghosts will be
her final legacy...
     and mine.

Gloria H. Procsal
Oceanside, CA

JUST TO EXIST

A moth was trapped between the window screen,
It fluttered up and down to find escape.
I watched its futile effort — so routine
That not a single inch was missed. It scraped
Soft fuzz from off its wings and yet it searche'd.
A curious bird investigates its move
And pecking at the screen — the moth did lurch
Towards the window pane, only to prove
Escape denied and it lay down to die.
As summer sun intensified, the heat
Compounding problems — 'til it would not try,
It struggled with its fate — it fought,
But in the end — its effort came to naught.

Darwynne Pucek
Kankakee, IL

YAMA, LORD OF DEATH

There is no escape from Him.
His decision is final.
His buffalo is no blind animal.
His noose knows its way.

Your fat savings in Swiss Banks,
your gold and diamonds in lockers,
can't bribe Him to shut his eyes.
No, not even a blank cheque duly signed.

Your prayers and prostrations,
your sweet-smelling flowers and joss sticks
can't tempt Him to grant you a reprieve.
No, not even a panegyric in pleasing verse.

The gruesome barrels of AK-47s
and the more sophisticated AK-56s
can't snap His all-powerful noose.
No, not even your acid bomb-shells.

Surrender, then, with a smile
writ large on your face.
Have no fear, no, not in the least,
for Yama is another Brahma.

P. Raja
India

MY ESCAPE

Sometimes I feel like escaping
And here's how I plan to execute it..
I'll cry...let my tears fall all around me,
Shower myself with my feelings,
Saturate myself in my emotions,
Indulge in an eternal, everlasting cry
That will remain forever in my soul.
As they slowly trickle down my cheeks,
They will absorb all impurities
And cleanse my heart of anger.
My Tears...My Escape.

Adela Rosa Ramos
North Miami, FL

SUMMER SUNDAYS

The whole clan gathered
At Bay Beach cove
A secluded niche
Known only to us natives

High tide filters water clean
For swimming
Then the hot sun
Dries our salty skin

Low tide
The muddy bottom
Teems with clams
We turn up big ones
For a chowder later
Little necks, half shelled
Cool in ice, sauce spiced
Slip between drooling lips

Labor Day which isn't Sunday
We climb
The close hill
In a Driftwood Derby
Competing for washed beauties
Moored on rocks
Lining the slope

Special pieces go home
Some to neighbors
Thin twigs, dry sea weed
Pit steam Driftwood Chicken,
Licking greasy fingers
We circle rising warmth
Chanting goodbyes
At open pit
As autumn nights nip nearer

Millie Raskin
Berkeley, CA

THE VASE

A butterfly, daisies, graceful leafy sprigs
Deeply cut into the glass.
The vase: tall, slim, firmly based,
Reflected rainbow-sparkling prismed light.
From its glassed-in shelf of proud exhibit,
It waited through winter for summer flowers.

Given to heal love's unyielding quarrel,
Sent as silent pleading,
Accepted in mutual forgiveness,
It had displayed the wedding roses.
"What a beautiful vase", the guests agreed,
As bride and groom rejoiced.

Through the years of spats and hugs and kisses,
Rose thorns etched scratches in the glass.
Noone these past twenty-five years
With whom to "kiss and make-up".
The aged spouse, independence lost,
Also waits for "summer".

She waits knowingly, contentedly, for the most part,
Though speech may not express that knowledge held.
Suddenly in her "winter" a sweet bouquet is brought.
"Oh! Such lovely flowers. Is that my vase?"
Even near blind eyes can sense
The vase's beauty valued so many years.

The soft white hands reach out, drawing it to her face;
She takes a long delighted inspiration of the flowers.
Feeling the cutwork, a hub for memories
Now long gone, but ever living.
As both the aged mother and only "child" recall them.

She wouldn't sell it, but curious
She'd asked an art appraiser. "Grand specimen!" he'd said.
"Too bad it's scratched; it has less value now."
But had it, as they, never known sharp thorns,
Specious beauty would it be.

Sister Francesca Reich, C.S.A.
Fond du Lac, WI

RAINBOWS

you stand inside me
fresh and alive
a spring rose
blooming
i wash you
with my tears
tell you
love is real
rainbows are lies
refracted
shattered light
my ears
absorb
the web
of your smile
tangled
we do not meld
we rip apart
and die
your words
are rainbows

Allen Renfro
Harriman, TN

CUT ROSES

Sensuous velvet buds blushing a deep red
are presented to me
together with a caring card
symbols of my students' appreciation.

I admire them in all their brilliant grandeur,
bring them home, place them in a vase,
watch petal after petal
leave the womb, unfold.

A week passes.
Their color dulls,
petals droop, drop,
expire on my table.

Only the card remains unchanged.

Ingrid Reti
San Luis Obispo, CA

ALL THINGS VISIBLE AND INVISIBLE

Oh, Holy Spirit! Dweller in my soul's impatient dreams
    (not of death, but of Dominion's winsome grace)
Acquaint me with the acquiescence that redeems
and make the time I touch a Holy Space.

And like a fragrance that inspects the ambient breeze
then fast discovers that it has no limit
    as it courts confluent seas
Let my comprehension span the mysteries in unknowing's sphere
    where still Your voice is heard
And lift my life above the weighty world
    to meet Your stunning Word!

Helen C. Rhodes
Saratoga Springs, NY

THE LITTLE RED CANISTER

She sat there serene,
with her hand on the canister,
as the ancestry looked on
from the wall near the banister.
The portraits told stories
of times long for-bye.

"A pair of mixed Cultures",
she went on to say,
"Has no one to turn to
to show them the way."

There sat the granddaughter,
tears filling her eyes.
"Can I really live
in the times gone-by?"

The image of him
and his forbidden embrace,
brought only fresh tears
to stream down her face.

"Matters of culture",
she thought for its part.
"Seem to have little
to do with the heart."

With a glance at the wall
and a thoughtful expression,
she concluded it wise
to proceed with discretion.

So she took some more tea
from the little red canister
as their faces stared down on her
high from the banister.

R. G. Rhymes
Japan

AUTUMN REFLECTION

I look out my window in amazement to see
Nature's lips in movement to share God-talk with me.

The warmth from strong sun-beams and brightness of today
Are gentle reminders that night has moved away.

Huge trees, swaying branches look like stately towers,
While winds breezing 'round them howl sounds of their powers.

The multi-colored leaves that beautify our earth
Soon leave their high abode to plan for a new birth.

Green grass once smooth, is burnt with blades now coated brown;
Harvest season signals that Winter's coming down.

All Autumn speaks of change with summer-breaking hands,
Portraying scenes of love in choicest colored strands.

How very much like life — this vision of the Fall;
God's everlasting love descends upon us all.

In Jesus, we receive deep warmth and healing light;
Pain and lonely moments move on as does the night.

'Tho joys and sorrows paint the leaves on each life's tree,
God's choice of colors blend inn perfect harmony.

When youthful health is worn through bodily ill and toil,
God's Own passionate care brings supernatural soil.

True growth requires much time and patience to mature;
God's Son endured long trial — to death for life secure.

Help me, Dear God, to bring this love-scene everywhere
And bless my Autumn life with thanks and praise-filled prayer.

Sister Marie Roccapriore, M.P.F.
Meriden, CT

LET THEIR VOICES REVERBERATE

Wordsmiths of Ancient Greece,
Ancient Rome, absorbing
the universe, the Deity
through wisdom's eyes
radiated beauty, love,
ethics, morality
through poetry, prose
that reigned higher than kings
on golden thrones
till forced to slide down
Rome's slimy decline
and lie in deep sleep
in long, dark valley of time
before aroused
to spread glow
all over the world,
captivating others
to match, coordinate visions,
generating culture
for hundreds of years...

Oh writers and poets of now—
of this downward, slithery age—
heed the cries
of Plato, Aristotal, Sappho,
Cicero, Horace.
Let their light
blaze on,
Let their voices reverberate,
let their voices reverberate.

Shirley Rodis
Coconut Creek, FL

THE GEORGE WASHINGTON BRIDGE

On the boat circling Manhattan you may travel
or stay home: its bored announcer will ignore
subtle flights of the dancer span crossing
New York and New Jersey, omit its reach
into mapless states. Strolling along its length I look

over into turquoise sparkle; up I look
at swaying harp string cables, travel
into self-lost listening. One can't ignore
this traffic beyond wheels: that which connects
shores of feeling moves one to a crossing

beyond clock - as with a tugboat crossing
jeweled through dark beyond my window. When I look
at its masked voyage I remember sleep connects
secrets in me, shaped into dreams that travel
out of my unknown. On that tour boat I ignore
announcer's prose. Nearing the span I reach

into questions: how build a bridge to reach
someone I've blindly hurt, make the crossing
over into another person? It's wise to ignore
single-span logic, Imagination must look
into double meanings for double travel,
grow bridges within my self. What connects

strangers in me can link with others, connects
surprise views of outsiders I can reach
by stretching out to touch. I must travel
beyond past eras in me, make the crossing
beyond ego, try not to ignore

terrain I've not outgrown. I must not ignore
my own river's opposite sides, must build what connects
my contraries. I can flow along, look
toward new places. I can make a crossing
over into ocean being, finally travel

beyond limited reach. Let that guide ignore
the subrler ways a bridge connects: crossing
under the span, I look into sparking travel.

Rose Rosberg
New York, NY

RON MC NAIR

Shocked, in disbelief the world donned a frozen stare;
Challenger was exploding, but barely in air;
The seven rugged astronauts perishing there
Included a black man, Ronald Erwin McNair.

He left his home, tiny Lake City, S.C.,
To attend North Carolina A & T;
The physic student, brilliant as one could be,
Went to MIT for his Doctorate degree.

Research scientists battles he earnestly fought;
Viewing valuable lessons he had learned and taught,
NASA picked him to become an astronaut;
For history he wrote an indelible part.

Hard-working, hard-playing and quite versatile too,
He wore a black karate belt; mean sax he blew;
Church teaching and counseling he made time to do;
To God, to humankind, he vowed to be true.

Shouldn't we note this devoted family man,
Whose wife and two children have proudly hailed him grand,
Was borned and reared in cotton and tobacco land
Where our ancestors built strong foundations that stand.

T'was a while ago, one chilly mid-winter day,
Mishap sprang instantly; he was taken away;
Then, though in deep mourning, we were mindful to say:
"For Ron's living and giving, Thank you, Lord we pray."

Ruth E. Royster
Roxboro, NC

POET'S LULLABY

Through the twist
of wisteria winding
we see her melodizing
as her window ripples
eventide with glare
of diamond daybreak
like the lighted buoy
that cleaves sea
during gales of storm.
The muse relaxes
into the circular back
of an aging feline
as its amanuensis
ostensibly chronicles
the world—
her point of contention—
penning then tugging
a strand of abundant hair
until the inspiration
lifts its aegis and moves
away jubilantly
like steam drifting
from cafe au lait.

Diana Kwiatkowski Rubin
Edison, NJ

ANN ELIZA
"I die of a broken heart"

Who was Ann Eliza, poet, savant,
daughter of Brandt Schuyler
and Margareta Van Wyck Schuyler,
later, wife of John Bleecker,
resident of Tomhanick on the
edge of wilderness and danger?

And why should we recall
or learn of her at all?

What happened to her beautiful blue ball
shoes and the muslins and lace left behind
that day as she journeyed such strange
pathways ahead of British and
Indians pursuing her peace?

The once New York belle
saw all her sweet beauty
turned now to hell.

Caught by death - mother sister, child—
lost; a husband fighting to hold fast
the freedom she would only know
by reading Homer, soothed by Virgil,
wanderers, as she, by hard paths.

An eighteenth century cameo,
living so briefly, in such cruel times;
whose loveliness still for all of us shines.

D. L. Rudy
Tenafly, NJ

RUNE

What she buried
in the red earth
another found
in a white dawn.

I thought it was a bird
but it's probably a woman
both of them almost gone
touching has worn
her down to stone
and clarity is gone
unless there is clarity in stone
and that is something different again.

Her feet are rough, still hurt to touch
breasts are palm shaped
she has become
a generality of form
which bothers me these days.

It was life she stayed for
what she could carve, could birth.

She stood tall once.

Now she is past
or a possibility
smudged
rounded
barely even stone
more its shadow.

Mary Kay Rummel
Fridley, MN

SUMMER '93

It hit like the Great Depression
rapidly, stalking all,
crushing with its burden
like the drop of Jericho's wall.
Pinned down by sweltering heat,
nothing to breathe but dust,
no rain clouds dot the horizon,
nothing to do but trust
that night will bring relief
and tomorrow will be better.
Next week shows and with it comes
a repeat, to the letter.
The mercury rises daily
and humidity begets sweat,
the Aged shelter from the sun
and mumble, swear, and fret.
Dustclouds strangle flowers
while Toadfrogs cower in fright.
The Jarfly claims the day
and Katydids choke the night.
At last comes a change in weather,
hope is fiercely mounting;
Summer, winded, and nearly out
is Down ...... Everyone is counting!

Paul Salyers
Olive Hill, KY

JOHNNY GREEN HILL

She said to me, "Sometimes you're very nice.
Why not always?" I said, "That's my true self.
The other one you see sometimes
is Johnny Green Hill."

That person I invented as a child
to terrorize my sister, some years younger.
"There's a mean guy," I said to her,
"named Johnny Green Hill

and he looks *just like me*. If he scares you
just call me right away, like Bob! Bob!
and I'll protect you from that mean guy,
Johnny Green Hill."

Then I'd leave the room. And come back in,
scowling fearsomely. Hands like claws.
"I'm gonna *get* you! Know who I am?
I'm Johnny Green Hill!"

Terrified, she'd scream, "Bob! Bob!"
I'd say, "Oh, I hear Bob coming! I'd better run!"
Then I'd rush out, and come back, but not
as Johnny Green Hill,

but as good old Bob to the rescue. "Where is he?" I'd shout,
"I'll beat him up! Trying to scare my sister!
I'm your brother Bob, I'll always protect you
from Johnny Green Hill."

I wonder if she remembers? She was only
about five, I guess. Hope not. To scare one's sister!
Sometimes, though, I scare myself
with Johnny Green Hill.

Robert Sargent
Washington, DC

VILLANELLE: MY SHORT HISTORY

We lived in a cold climate: no one
died for love. Somehow the days
slid by. At times we saw the sun

and once, we made a garden: stone
and lichen. Paths an icy maze.
Our blood ran cold. Slowly, one

by one, some froze. No place to run!
Who burned our woods? Legend says
a mushroom cloud blew out the sun.

I dreamt of warm currents: an ocean
gently spun in a silken haze.
But life locked in. A wintery one

twisting in my bones like iron.
My cold companion flamed. The blaze
consuming, challenged the honeyed sun

at noon. Somehow the cold won.
Sometimes I loved the snowman's gaze.
In that charged air, he was the one
I claimed. You had to imagine the sun.

Helen Saslow
Chestertown, NY

THE SONG OF LIFE

They rise up our of silence,
the first soft notes of Life's beginning.
Through a waiting stillness sing
the simple chords of growth, awareness,
filling empty space with primal melody.

The song, in harmony and discord,
rises in a hastening crescendo.
Chords, growing in complexity and depth,
develop, changing, endlessly recurring
becoming first a fugue, then an enigma.

The song, a celebration,
cymbals crashing in an ecstasy of triumph.
Drums, echoing Life's heartbeat.
The song, a requiem, a lament,
chanting, sobbing in a minor key.

Then the coda, largo and diminuendo,
gentle, broken, feeble chords,
Life's first and final notes repeating.
Softer, ever softer, even softer
until all, again, is silence.

Sheila Saunders
Juno Beach, FL

A TRIBUTE TO MY MOTHER

She was pretty, petite and smart.
I was proud of her accomplishments,
Her just decisions and her love from the heart.

Her goal was to study, and teach.
To educate people for work, and living,
To continue grasping for what is just beyond one's reach.

Mom rarely spoke of the past.
Ancestors, and complaints, were of little concern.
She anticipated tomorrow, thoughts new, knowledge to last.

She's gone now, but we're not parted.
Her spirit makes me chuckle when I feel it say,
"If you think something should be done, get started."

Harriet Schaeffer
Cortland, NE

TREASURE HUNT

Do you travel through your life
Seeking its hidden treasure?
Would you cast aside all strife
When adversity adds to your measure?

Sadness and sorrow will come and go.
But, good times will be there, too.
You'll have some friends, and perhaps a foe,
Who will either support or test you.

Do fame and riches spell success?
Then you need to look deep inside.
A peaceful heart brings happiness
When your conscience is your guide.

Faithful love is to be cherished.
And hard work deserves some leisure.
Don't waste your time on foolish wishes
Because, life itself is the treasure.

Elaine M. Schaid
Chicago, IL

ON BEING TOLD OF MY DAUGHTER'S ENGAGEMENT

Two children.
Unaware
of future
obstacles.

Which will corner them.
Ensnarle them.
Even possibly destroy them.

At the very least
change them.

Sit.
and shrug.
and ask
for blessings.

Jacklon Schmidt
Lincoln, NE

CLAMOR

When you looked out the window
what did you see that day?
Did the afternoon shadows obliterate
the quiet symmetry of the landscape?
What did you hear?
Did the anarchist voices in your head
triumph at last?
Psychiatrists,
the chemicals to balance the imbalance
filed.
The pain you bled into your poems
couldn't mute the voices,
couldn't erode the memories.
So, often they seated you
in the padded white blankness
that screamed to you
for the adornment of images.

The slashes,
the red flow that afternoon
paralyzed only your body, not your mind.
Now, your tongue an anchor,
you lay motionless
in hospital sheets.
The babel of voices
and ricocheting images
held behind eyes
that view white ceiling in daylight
and blackness at night.

Death eluded you,
taking only your poetry.

Jeanne Leigh Schuler
Corte Madera, CA

FROM MOUNT OLYMPUS

The waters of Greece
are so blue, rocks so old,
Sculptures ageless.
Sun beats down on antiquity,
the clock turns slowly...
Mules trudge island streets.
Hydrofoils race between
castles that were built,
crumpled and rebuilt.
Olympia, Delphi and Delos
stand sacred on their soil.
Awe whispers in the waves
that lap the shores.
Fishermen bring home
their catch and nets.
Sameness presses against
the passage of time.
Beneath the Agean sky
the Greek Philosophers
watch contentedly.

Ruth Wildes Schuler
Novato, CA

NIGHT AT THE POND

Under the stars
in the still night
the small pond
where the frogs have
the audiences of the fresh starts.
They do not need to live long
can give their songs one summer only
and then stay
in some listener's soul
who had that just one night
to stand there
thinking of infinite things,
and feeling.

We need not
worry so much about each other.
Everyone has some moment
when there was eternity
just for himself or herself —
though perception is different for each
and each word must be said
slowly, deliberately
not rushed through embarrassedly
as if to take care of all
the grammar quickly.

It's something to have
a night alone beside a small pond
and something infinite to remember
for all eternity, encountered there

beside the late summer weeds
and star stirred gossamer
winds.

We are all billionaires
No one is poor at all on this vast
earth.

Sister Mary Faith Schuster, OSB
Atchison, KS

PAST A CHILD

Susie!
At the start of
an adventure.
Susie!
Still is not sure
what to make of it.

You have
heard all kinds of things
from this and that
and every other one
who's got it.

Not all
of what you hear is
positive and pleasing
to you.

Susie,
nonetheless,
but slow and sure,
you're entering the
fringe of womanhood.

Susie,
knowing you,
why anything that tags
along with growing up,
will be much welcomed.

Deloris Selinsky
Shavertown, PA

JEMEZ SPRINGS, NEW MEXICO

morning

tall elms sift down
the paper pennies of old bloom
the paper coins of their seed

noon

in high
green branches
of the cottonwoods

angels touch down
dissolve

move on

sunset

light from the river
dazzles the flecked air

and stars crack open
in the poplar trees

night

shadowy water
water
watersound

all
night long
the lulling
river

Jeanne Shannon
Albuquerque, NM

HOMAGE TO DYLAN THOMAS

Whores who came to buy your songs, Dylan, stayed to sing them.
Dylan..never were you bought. You could not be sold.
Large winged birds, pebbled brain dumb, flying clean heavens
Happier than you, Dylan. Lonely, bleeding mouthed poet.
Oh Dylan. Hurling imagery. Moses. Solomon. Boy. In love with life,
Giant Dylan. Larger than the dollar signs. Wee ants. Don't hears.
Muffled, who made sport of you.

You flew across our firmament, Dylan, a meteor.
I weep, Dylan. I hurt, for brown whiskeys breaking your brain,
Spilling blood your mouth, never spoiling your songs,
To buy your pearls in New York. Dylan! Poisoned by bad weathers,
Witch doctors invented medicines, yellow-blue-sad
To silence the sensitives. To separate body from soul.
Tho they break us with hemlock, the death pieces gather.
Singing voices you gave to the deaf dumb and blind.
The stench of six million Jews, Dylan. Schumann burns gas chambers.
Van Ghogh, Dylan and Chausson. Marilyn Monroe labeled sex, wronged.
Rabbi Akiba, poet of the Bible, tortured, unbroken
As they peeled off his thin skin. With faith his skinny bones
Chanted the Shema. "SHEMA YISROAEL ADENAI ELOHENU, ADENAI
    ECHUD."
"I AM ONE WITH MY LORD. MY LORD MY GOD IS ONE." Oh deaf. Oh
    dumb.
Oh blind, unspoken. Cry anger, Dylan! Joan of Arc listening
To the voices of God. Dylan...who listens the voices that
Cry the still night?

Dylan....unripe the generations.
Now come the women in the metamorphosis of centuries long gone.
We walk with you...Dylan, all women. And saints march slowly....
        one......by......one
Dylan....you are not alone.

Rose Sher
New York, NY

THE DOLPHIN

Just off the Santa Monica Pier,
a dolphin swam in tight circles
for hours, having lost its power
to echolocate a wiser course.

No matter that photographers,
marine biologists, and reporters
with their mini-cams and prayers
tried to will it from its torment:

the dolphin churned and turned
with dizzy ardor, as if devotion
to repetition could set it straight,
could help it navigate to freedom.

Was it toxins spewed in the ocean
that sent its brain to spinning,
or do dolphins, just like humans,
go off the deep end, either with

or without reason? Exhausted,
finally, the dolphin drowned.
On t.v. it looked as still as time.
But it keeps circling in my mind.

Maurya Simon
Mt. Baldy, CA

THE JEWEL

Lost in time.
Lost forever, can't be found.
A jewel undiscovered for years.
Soon to be uncovered by the sand.
Treasured as an ancient relic.
Precious and rare.
Only those who take the time to look can see what is unique about this stone.
The shape, color, and value.
It sparkles as the sun reflects off its many facets.
Revealed is a tiny ball contained inside the jewel which holds the secret to its never-
    ending power.
Only if you find the key will that secret power be revealed to you.
Only then will you truly understand the importance of the jewel.

Stephanie Sinclair
Louisville, KY

RECOLLECTIONS

She sits beside her window rocking,
Gently rocking to and fro,
Wondering why her thoughts dwell fondly
On that day so long ago.
The morning sun shone on the water,
The birds sang sweetly in the pines,
Love came quietly, warmly, tenderly,
Enrapturing their puerile minds.
Time hurts and heals and passes quickly,
And memories dim as one grows old,
But time cannot erase a picture
Etched in one's mind and framed in gold.
She sits beside her window rocking,
Gently rocking to and fro,
Thankful for this lingering picture
Instilling yet an ardent glow.

Murdena C. Skinner
Canada

MY LOVE IS AN IMMENSITY

So close, it sat upon my shoulder
and I wondered why
a thing so fragile and so shy
a perfect butterfly

would land here
in such a scarey place,
What lesson do you teach me, Lord?
Was this your grace

gently touching me
until I cry?
"Yes, my love is grander
than a butterfly."

I saw the majestic maple tree
draped in green ecstacy.
She waved her leafy arms at me.
"My love is taller than a tree."

I watched the wind caress the sea
It was so fresh and free.
It spoke this word to me,
"My love is an imensity."

I knew by the tears upon my cheek,
your love overwhelms the weak.
I knew I could not be the same
because your love has called my name.

I know that deep inside of me
there burns a great intensity,
a longing to be free
to love you as you love me.

Sister Virginia Skrdlant, S.H.C.J.
Rosemont, PA

YESTERYEAR'S CHILD

I painted the child who once was I =
she came to life with a rainbow tune,
Holding so tightly her red balloon,
While her white cat looked on and the
    rose tree grew,
And what treasures the black-eyed susans saw,
    no grown up ever knew;
And the mushroom was at the door of a
    dance hall
Where fairies and elves had a
    gala ball,
And the dewdrops were diamonds and the sun's rays
    were gold,
She came to life that child of old,
And whispered a secret to me:
Can you guess how to be as happy as she?

Mary McGowan Slappey
Washington, DC

RAIN

Through the damp February streets
The puddles glitter with neon reflections.
Forests of car lights blaze through the highways
Leading everywhere, going nowhere.

Sheets of icy silver shimmer like diamonds.
Curtains of gray fog the windowpanes.
Is it shrouds from the grave lifted upwards?
Is it tears from the heavens showering praise?

Ripples of reflections, the past and the future,
Soaring to the heights, plunging to the depths.
From above, come the droplets to nourish the oceans.
So flows the waters of spirit to mankind below.

Liz Sleckman
Wantagh, NY

SUBURBAN CREDO

In our soft peignoirs we recollect
our years of practising the pre-arranged
in kitchen, bath and bed—
what is correct
and programmed long before our lives were changed
by bombs and cures.
We scan this new society—
its buried missiles
and longer span to care.
It puts to test the piety
we nurtured toward our men when love began.
And yet suburban Eve still works like hell
to clean this pleasant planet,
clear the skies,
and weed the gardens
even since she fell.
Tradition would not have it otherwise.
So
pack your feelings in a bed of ice.
What we are doing, ladies,
will suffice.

Mary Wren Small
Wilmette, IL

PERFECT
for Jerome Ward

Preparing the salad,
you said the word
"perfect" in botany

denotes a species
bisexual and self-sufficient,
while we cut carrot

roots, inflorescence
of broccoli, the ripened
ovaries of olive

and bulb of the red
onion Every seed,
you said, holds

an embryo inside. It's
all so simple, and we call
plants primal because

they survive without
devouring one another
and often work their

increase alone. Still, we
never envy the spiral
of cabbage leaves or

a potato's albino eye,
as "perfect" comes from
the Latin for "complete,"

and we prefer this
process of emerging,
two imperfect men

happily whittling dinner
for their loved ones,
as windblown pollen

dusts the windows, our
bright knives clicking
on the board.

R. T. Smith
Auburn University, AL

THE LAST BEE-ROBBER

The young men of the village
    would sooner dance through knives
Than risk the ballet of the cliff-face.

But they will meet with little smiles
    and nudges; hand him down
His sack, his goggles and his smoker.

He's seen, on the village TV,
    lean and bronze-thewed men
A-bounce on *cordes du rappel.*

But he knows, with eyes tight-shut,
    every vine and tree-root,
Every wary swallow's nook.

The combs he takes with bee-lumped hands
    hold honey sweeter than
The sticky jars in the bodega.

The Sun's warmth on his back cannot
    push off the Earth's chill fingers
On his chest; a foretaste of

The day the years of bee-venom
    will finally reach his heart
And dry him to a bas relief,

    A guardian glyph for bees.

Robert L. Smith
New York, NY

THESE DAYS, THE SWAMP MAPLE

Outside my window
the swamp maple hangs its red pouched seedbags

before full leaves come,
and the envelopes carrying the hard, ready seed.

Junk tree, weed of the high places, first flower
half mimosa in color,

how blousy these red velvet blossoms
against the neighbor's shingle roof and blue sky.

The bark of the sinewy trunk
is very black,

the fine leaves, when they come,
edged jagged.

Each spring the first droppings are like earth itself
dumping onto our cars parked

in the shared gravel drive.
There is nothing delicate in this,

the red mud, leonine shapes,
manes and haunches,

interrupting the smooth hood's black.
Small seeded rosettes are clear in the splotches,

layered forms, along with the color,
despite the litter.

The second round of pink, veined, translucent
wings holding the seed

boomerangs over the patio and lawn,
leafleting the cause of life, abundance, risk

in a call to sweep and sweep.
I cannot give up yet the tension between mess

and loveliness, after rain,
on the most ordinary April morning.

Elizabeth Anne Socolow
Grosse Pointe Park, MI

POETRY

Words bled from flesh and bone ..
these flow, extend and dance,
and like the sun, enhance
and make life shine.
A poet's words: not relics
but a shrine
to one who senses life.
Poetry's a marrowness
that feeds and girds one's soul-bone
in its truth,
connects it to the hip-bone
to the thigh bone,
up and down
from there.
A soul can bounce and bound in air
if there's a poem in the bone;
can touch earth
lightly
as a robin's notes
breezily
as wind-blown tumbleweed
gently
with a hand on a sagging should r
an arm around the waist.

Wilma Spellman
Park Ridge, IL

HOTEL HIDALGO
NOCHISTLAN
ROOM SIX

It doesn't matter what time it is
It's always the same time
In this room with no windows
Only the sounds of an unhappy baby and barking dog
Reach us funnelled down the air shaft
In this room of eternal night
That dog is a trained barker
I wonder about the baby
The alarm goes off at 9AM
It's still the middle of the night
The baby and the dog still up
For a full day of screaming and barking
To no one who cares

John Wiley Stack
Santa Barbara, CA

A TEACHER'S LAMENT

He came, little Tom, in tattered clothes—
hands unwashed and unwiped nose.
"Readin' I hate and hist'ry, too...
In fact, teacher, there ain't much I can do."
... and I called him a Potential Failure.

Linda, young with street-wise eyes
hostile, sassy, a thousand whys
"I don't believe... I hate... I doubt...
Can't wait for June 'til I get out!"
... and I wished for June, too.

And Gary whose god was the football field
used his prowress as a constant shield—
"Why strain my head on Trig or Chem?
I've got it made at U of M."
... and I knew he was a show-off.

Oh, that Danny! He drove me mad!
A little old man with a face stamped SAD.
"My Ma don't like me... the kids are mean...
school's the dumbest place I seen."
... and I said he just didn't try.

Now the years have passed and I'm all alone...
I wonder where Tom and the others have gone
and the books I cherished lie covered with dust;
the once shiny bell is eaten with rust.
... and, God, how I miss them!

How I'd love to turn back those hurried years,
inspire your hearts and calm your fears—
and offer the wisdom mere books don't possess
and tell you, each one, *"I must confess*
... I need you!

"For I, too, am human, a student like you—
I"ve failed many tests as all of us do...
so let's start, not as teacher and pupil, but rather
*as **friends** who struggle and travel ... TOGETHER!"*

Sister Ann Stamm
Livonia, MI

GOOD NEWS
"He is Risen."
To Karen Lillard

This morning's ground fog,
  the rising Morning Star
    primrose-yellow Denver sun-rays
      and a May day splashed with crystal dew

dabbed Miss Minervia's
memorial hedge of rosebushes
with broad yellow brush strokes
of glowing Texas Roses.

Richard Stepsay
Denver, CO

ARACHNE

Spread like thin linen fragments
Over frail branches of privet, cedar, cypress,
Webs trap insects small as a pore or a pinpoint.
Their infinitesimally veined, transparent wings
Flutter, tensing and testing strands weighted by
Water globules awash with invisible life.
Over these, the wing-caught, the water-swimmers,
Presides the spider, unseen.

Somewhere near stickily cemented joinings,
Far-stretched, high wire connections,
Waits the weaver, the watcher, the creator-destroyer.
Beneath a branch shadow, a rain splatter, a slow-unfurling leaf,
The spider is hiding, the spider is resting, the spider is planning
Nighttime excursions of inspection and ingenious expansion,
Designs that may be destroyed by chance in an instant
Or remain suspended for many spider days.

Where is the spider? Is the spider coming?
Will she succor the struggling, suspended by a mere mandible?
Will she unwrap the silent ones waving stiffly in the updrafts?
Where *is* the spider? Pray spider, show yourself.
Reveal your far-seeing eyes, your foaming jaws.
We are dazzled by your artistry, paralyzed by your miracles.
Now it is you we crave as we wait in suspension,
Hanging from threads and crying: "Show us your transfiguring face."

Elisabeth Stevens
Baltimore, MD

TEACHER

Please teach me what it is You see
And help me see it, too.
And whatever pleases Thee,
Help me, that, to do.

Grant me certain victory
To win the long, hard race.
Help me give it all I've got
Until I see Your face.

So easy is it to despair
But I will not give up.
I've come this far and now I know
My prize will be the cup.

Linda J. Stewart
Canada

THE HERMIT WINTER

The hermit winter, hidden from Autumn
Blasted her ruby leaves
With a frosty aggression
He blackened her gowns sleeves.

In his howling winds he would serenade
Songs to prophecy her doom
He said sleep, my darling Autumn
Inside my icy tomb.

I'll bed you down in lacy white
With trim of satin ice
Your outspoken beauty
Always was my greatest vice.

Your long flowing locks of hair
Frocked in flaming boldness
Let me put your fire out
I'll fill you with my coldness.

So with a sigh Autumn slept
And winter won the war
But waiting ahead to melt his heart
Sunny spring stood at the door.

Narda R. Strong
Churubusco, IN

NATIONAL DEBT

If you get credit for a crime
falsely served,
can you apply that credit
to a crime successively executed?
For example:
You are accused of murdering
your wife.
Twelve years later, your lawyer
proves you were innocent.
They let you out.
Everyone bends over backwards
to make amends.
You get a good job at the brewery.
And marry the Boss's daughter.
She's a dog in bed.
You kill her.
The Boss dies of grief.
You are his only heir
and inherit the business.
You get off on accidental homicide
and are sentenced to twelve years.
But wait,
they credit your account.

Roberta Swann
New York, NY

NOTHING NEW

The world on which we are guests
is ruled only by thieves.
Thieves rule this world.
They silence the birds and the children,
Steal our earth, water, air,
sell us gas masks and advertise
the conquest of space.

They steal our renaissance, humanism, romanticism
and when we complain to the Better Business Bureau,
an answering machine with an artificial voice says:
"please leave your number."
Yes, they steal our oil and ozone and blood and sweat
with which they build
their feudal capitalism.

The world on which we are guests
is dominated by thieves.
Thieves rule this world;
steal our arteries, guts, hemoglobin,
our eyes and ears, our souls and bodies,
our sunrises and sunsets;
and sell us cholesterol, stress, and cancer of the colon.

The thieves swindle us; they know
we are helpless with their laws and constitutions.
They steal our spouses and process them into
antibiotic and hormone contaminated meat,
and probably the only things they leave us
are death, taxes, and ever pricier
holes in swiss cheese.

This is the world on which we are guests.
This is the life of which we are constantly robbed.

Adam Szyper
Kendall Park, NJ

LOOKING AT GOLDEN GATE BRIDGE
(for Michael Barchoff Glick 1946-1983)

You told friends who called that morning, "Can't
talk now. Something I have to do." As
though going to the store, you put
ID in your pocket and went out.

    In water   made hard   as stone
        by height   you met   your face

Like a scene in someone else's life,
I catch myself watching and slowly
turn where sunlight stretches your absence
along budding limbs, twinning shadows.
              *

Your hands were bloodless Indian pipes,
candles in their box. Blood sounded
in my ears as I stiffly forced myself
to lean across white satin and kiss

your pale cheek as though I had never
breathed its warmth or tasted its smoothness.
It's painful to see your smile with Dad's
on a photo where you plant for spring.
              *

Seated on a child's toilet seat,
giggling, frowning, imitating me.
Bigger, his Boy Scout knife scared
three toughs who wanted his paper route money

which he later used to buy my first TV
when I got married, "so you could see
there were good things on TV."
He was coming out of the water,

out of a dream, and his skin was so cool
I couldn't touch it. He was as
white as sky, as fog before my face
fading at a touch. Yet he was there,

pure of himself, empty pockets, just
a driver's license to bring him to
the edge of this world, organ donor card
to carry him into the next.

Marilynn Talal
San Antonio, TX

THE WEAKER SEX

WOMAN
   bent over a washing board
as faded and worn as the clothing.
Back and heart too strong
to let the body go
its own way.
Hanging on
even God does not know
why
her time has come and gone
many times
   the first baby
labor endless like Sisyphus pushing
that stone and pushing but
getting nowhere   the baby stillborn
then
there was the winter of snow
and cold freezing the world
on it axis pneumonia became a word
whispered in many rooms
still the breath
would not leave her altogether
and now
the cancer
weaving itself into her clutching
at her like a fearful child.
She does not resent it
a mother gives and gives until
she is empty and her child
is full.

Conciere Taylor
Flushing, NY

MAGIC MIRRORS

At the age of sixty-four
I wish for magic mirrors
To blow out all the candles
    of all the golden years.
As the light grows dim
I look again and then....
I see the years as they swiftly fly
like birds at winters end.
I long to recall the past
just to review the hopes and dreams
of a future clear and bright
but my magic mirror reflects so plain
the misfortunes of my life.
No, no I cry as I view the past I
must not look back, I must look to
the future for I am not old yet.
Oh magic mirror how thoughtless how my spirit
does explain, you are my soul
what God hath made, yes no one can deny
A magic mirror cannot describe nor change
A mortal such as I

Josephine Copenhaver Thomas
Prescott, AZ

FROM MANILLA — FUGUE TO A MARTYR

Christ: How fare my valleys, how fare my roads?

Angel: Rizal passed upon first light.
In Paco Park his marker glows.

Two Choruses:
Bullets flew into a spirit nearing night;
upon a flame that tore the form
to hearts ignite!

O humble cross on a bed of spring sent flowers;
Rizal did lay beneath thee,
embracing Liberty.

Angel: Behold the Man—

Choruses: Christ it was Who bled upon the dead,
bestowing Life—as Rizal dying bled.

The sun implodes dawn's fragile night;
Rizal walks from shadows, shivering Light.

Angel: My tears are silent fallen.

Choruses: Did typhoons scream on that day;
uprooting trees—cascading, flayed!

Or was the whisper of one shy dove
the only sound that met his love?

Angel: Married night the priest pronounced you dead;
thy tears of love engulfed her quaking dread.

Christ: I rise. Philippine passes before the nations.

Choruses: Come dream within that waiting time
when earth will bound, embracing Love;
And Christ will walk with peasant bride
upon these lanes that Rizal trod.

Tony Thomas
Alameda, CA

I'M SO HAPPY I COULD DANCE

It doesn't take so very much
Of material things in life
To make my eager heart rejoice
As I hurdle every strife.

Every day is but a bonus
If we strive to do our best
For it's the "little things in life"
That adds beauty in our quest.

I find beauty in the sunshine
And deep velvet of the night,
There is peace in golden sunsets
That I find a sheer delight.

How I love the Hope and *Promise*
That unfolds at break of day
When the tiniest little flower
Has a message to convey.

I thank God for my loyal friends
And for garden's patchwork quilts.
My heart keeps dancing with such joys
Balancing on spirit stilts.

Yes, I'm so happy I could dance
Just to be alive each day
And I pray I may help others
To find beauty on their way.

Kathleen Irene (Katie) Tibbetts
Minneapolis, MN

ANN ELIZA (SCHUYLER) BLEECKER (1752-1783)

"Alas, the wilderness is within"
Ann Bleecker did proclaim
As she penned her words through poetry
And novels which became
A descriptive part of history
(SURVIVAL being one's aim.)

Yet, the terror of her frontier life
Did not destroy her zeal
For her love of land and human life ...
Or PROVIDENCE ... to heal
As she penned her thoughts which would in time
Portray just how she'd feel.
She was born in New York city
In Seventeen, Fifty-Two
And from her early childhood years
Loved books and writing too.

When she married at age seventeen
She destroyed the notes that she had penned
For the roles a wife and mother lend.

Encouraged by her husband, John,
A lawyer of great wealth,
She started in to write again
Despite her fragile health.
They settled in Tomhanich town
Not far from Albany
Where natural scenes she wrote so well
Were her identity.
Her feelings were "Wordsworthian"
It often has been said,
But form and style were her own
(Ann Bleecker was well read.)
When we think of all she had endured
That didn't destroy her zeal
We find courage and the qualities
Ann Bleecker's words reveal.

Laurene J. Tibbetts
Minneapolis, MN

FORSAKEN CLUE

Palavis, back to visit Thessaly,
clumps up mountain cemetery snow
to where his grandparents' ancestors were buried
to tell them now he knows what they so long
knew. He sits, his back to a tree, sleeps.

His old ones spring out, "har, har," they joke
in breath balloons, "come join us in the dance
and feast." "But I have no handkerchief for the dance,
that old custom." Below his hand a handkerchief
appears on snow. He gasps, grabs it, dances
wildly, feasts, a great clatter is there
as everyone talks, catches up.

A winter storm claps forth and his back unsticks
from the tree. All is a dream, he knows, standing.
He slaps off some snow from his mitten and there is the
handkerchief. His eyes widen, breath is held, then is
let go as he shakes his head slowly. "I'm not spirit-prone,
I have sought too long, no answer on that phone,
zip, zero zed. As he walks back down
he says again,

"where can my old ones be found
to tell them now I know what they so long knew
that children grow and when do they grow
and where can my old ones be found."

Ellen Tifft
Elmira, NY

YOUNG AGAIN

Drapery cleaners come early
I play the piano as I wait
They knock, come in smiling
say they like the sound.
One set up a ladder climbed
to unhook drapery pleats.
The other passed my cluttered table.
He stopped to pick up a clipping,
"Did you cut this out?" he asked
as he lifted up a photo of a spider web.
I nodded, "I just wrote a spider poem."
I write poetry too," he answered.
With that he rolled up his sleeve
elbow high to reveal a spider web tattoo.
I could only murmur, handed him my poem.
He read, said, "Good." He rattled
off a last line for this poem,
a metaphor that pulled the ending tight.
"Do you paint, too? Some poets do."
"No, but I sew. See those stuffed animals."
He gave each one a pat, looked back at me,
"You know I could marry you."
The animals stared out with button eyes.
He aged forty, more or less,
A tattooed drapery hanger
I, an "old-old" lady with a pen and pins
Both busy in a world of day to day
Both also poets spinning fragile, complex webs.

Mildred Toogood
Laguna Hills, CA

IMAGINATION'S PRIEST
For William Stafford

He walks into the temple of learning with the words he's written
while the dawn wrote the morning light.
I offer him my own words as though they are prayers.
They fall to the floor, a clutter of papers not in order.
A priest of the imagination, he bends to help me pick them up.
I hear the echo of a line he wrote somewhere:
"You must kneel down and explore for them."
This kneeling down together absolves my embarrassed soul.

Patricia Ann Treat
Bremerton, WA

FATHER

Build your house on solid rock and many storms it will withstand,
But take heed for what will happen if your house is built on sand.

The waves will crash against it and force it to the sea,
Until the traces of its existence are nothing but debris.

So too within a marriage the father must be sure
His house has a solid foundation or it will never endure.

The partner he is given is the blueprint of the plan,
Because God knew the strength of woman would give courage to the man.

And he passes to his children the wisdom of his years,
He holds their hands when they are small and comforts all their fears.

And when his work is over and time he can enjoy
A foundation of love he has built that nothing can destroy.

Patricia Truscello
Tewksbury, MA

SOMETIMES

you, are forever lost to me

sometimes, just sometimes
Mediterranean waters
shimmer before me
as your eyes did
that night

and sometimes, just sometimes
I feel the old rage
crackling,
fading to ember
remembering you,

forever lost, to me

Sonia Usatch
Brookhaven, NY

HUMILITY OF THE LORD

How humble was the Lord who
washed the feet of his disciples, and,
then, towelled them. They,
then, cried,
what he was doing. He said,
he was teaching the lesson of humility.

He forgot himself to the welfare of mankind.
Hunger and thirst were not the impediments
on his ways. While
hills and rocks gave him ways.
He walked the cobbled and thorny roads
day and night cheerfully.

He welcomed the
laughters and abuses of
the ignorant pagans with humbleness.
He also answered their
javelin questions with gentleness.

They were/are proud of forgetting the
coming hour of their death.

Y. N. Vaish
India

AND THEN

Remember Tennyson's lines when my soul's fled,
    "And may there be no moaning of the bar..."
No, sing Te Deum in remembrance of the dead;
    The tattered soul released from this world's wars.
The tears of grief you shed, let them be understood
    As for your pain at our parting in this life.
Let it be known that the new state of my soul is good
    And God's giv'n me a respite from the strife.

Howard Van Dine
Bristol, VT

BEAUTY SPOT

This is a scene of beauty!
  Each year's blooms seem the loveliest ever.
Such a peaceful place delights my heart.
  In the stillness are seen God's wonderful works of nature.

The majestic pines, the hill covered with golden daisies
  Entwined with little red flowers below the blue and white sky
    Each working out an individual charm of grace.

I softly whisper my prayers in the silence
  Near this contemplative place with God.
This restful solitude fills my heart with radiance of God's art,
  O Lord, I thank you forever!

Sister Mary of the Visitation
West Springfield, MA

STEPS AND COFFINS

In over-stuff rooms caricatures of life
move numbly to an unhearing voice.
Capitally precise like a clock in a telegraph office
they are sure of the hour,
the future is to them a time-punch.
Knowing that doors open to cold winds
they have accepted death as a regular fellow
insuring themselves for at least a grave.
Death comes, clocks click
clerking the seconds these men are.
Insolently as worms fertilizing earth
their backs grow skyscrapers
like spikes Godward sending their dead souls.
They have become stairs fate has made flesh,
the coffins their souls are in are stairs
rising step by step until their souls sleep
like discarded levers accepting ease
as an intermission to their unnovel use.
Sleep is sweet. Death comes in mood too sweet
for men strung in their muscles like strained wires.
Men die..death is a platitude mingling with hopes.
Death untouches all like a shadow of a hand seen and gone.
In shrill whistles of fate they are capering drills
dancing into stone doors.
They are steel snakes embracing households.
Love has become a giant throwing knives
into the thumping motors of their flesh.
Speechless are their voices.
Tired without thoughts their minds.

Sigmund Weiss
Stony Brook, NY

AN UNKINDNESS OF RAVENS

The pheasant had been killed
by a blizzard, its head
matted with ice, encased
in an absurd lacquer.

All around it sat
an unkindness of ravens,
a collection of ravenous moments
pulling up meat.

Except one, sitting apart,
the white bowls of its eyes
full of half-eaten prey.
But when it flew,

driven like an impulse
toward an indefinite nerve end,
for a moment the snow's
dead flesh was alive.

Don Welch
Kearney, NE

NAPKIN DISPOSAL

So neat in the stall: the sanitary
Mail-drop for the monthly installments
We pay to be fertile; secretly here,
The cyclical blood-lettings and blood—
Staunchings that vary for each with her moon.
On the wall, where aumbries squirrel
The necessities of these menses, mirrors image
The doors and the faces emergent: the virginal,
The matronly, late-menopausal, fresh-napkined
For filling each role. With no ritual
Of cleansing now, the dutiful lore of protection
Passes from mother to daughter, woman to girl,
In privy counsels: how to repair this feminine
Wound, how to appear always winged even wearing
The cocoon pearled with blood, how, when outgrown,
To cherish the past arcane rhythms of having
Been butterfly, butterflew, butterflown.

Nancy G. Westerfield
Kearney, NE

CORNISH, NEW HAMPSHIRE

There are, in America, places removed
from disaster, where houses sit on their view
of the mountains, so blue they seem painted on skies,
where lawns spread their aprons in shade, and cars
come home like the cows returning from pasture.
Not a soul. An interior life broods. All the doors
are left open, the keys in the locks, and the roads
unused, unwinding like yawns. It is late
in the day, light lapping up all the gold.
Trees, like their owners, are arrogant here,
each one on its own, with a trunk climbing straight
to its limit. Through coniferous darkness
the breeze walks overhead. Frogs plunk into pools
of muddy black water. A dragonfly weaves
a blue dance. Holidays are like this,
an illusion of emptyness filled to the brim
with a resinous fever of insects, waiting
to strike, news droning on dead telephones.

Claire Nicolas White
St. James, NJ

THE PRICE OF A TRAIN RIDE

Trains sound like drunks having a bad dream.
Ten o'clock at night, clocks are stained by free whiskey.
Ad posters half absorbed in urinary fellowship
peel onto the paths of pedestrians distracted by schedules.
The subway system moves like a tongue after the slaughter.
The cars are crowded by owls of many nations,
who have come to ride the big dream
cities are supposed to hold in the purse of their streets.
It was a crowded car and tonight was special,
not because a young man dozed after work,
nor a boring ride that offered poor ventilation
and unlawful occupancy. He slept like a piece of wood
riding the waves while a teenage girl
lit the man's hair and face.
Conscientious passengers flagged the flames out
in time to save the man's life and vision.
The girl betrayed by friends was charged
on several counts while someone else threatened
to puncture strangers with a hyperdermic needle
containing aids contaminated blood, all for
the price of a token non stop in our
semi-anarchistic state and sorrow. The meeting hall for
apologies and union strikes, won't make a better
ride for the money. Call that sports spectacular.
We do not say we are always profound,
polished like sterling silver, a gleam sharper than mirrors,
but at what age does one develop appetites of anger
and indifference to drive a girl to set a human torch
while another hollers, "I've got aids, and I'm going to
puncture you with my tainted blood?!" Several civilizations
ago the Alexandrian, Brachium, Serapeum libraries were
destroyed, lost were seven hundred thousand scrolls, all for
parasite, the ingredients, one cup of indifference, two cups
of negligence and even as we speak part of our nation's
damaged records are floating up the creek.

Mildred Wiackley
New York, NY

WHAT HAS XIV WCP DONE TO ME
Monterrey, Mexico Aug. 19-23, 1993
XIV World Congress of Poets

Nestled 'neath mountain peaks,
     misty clouds encircling us,
We poets come to gather in unity
     of asking world leaders
To demonstrate a new education
     raising new hope in hearts
Of our children:

MEXICO spread your welcoming us—
To every nation to emulate you—
So all nations, seek a brotherhood,
And a peace through their poets, too.

Rosemary C. Wilkinson
Placerville, CA

MISSA BREVIS IN F - K-192, MOZART

typical this

Wolfie's playfulness
Wolfgang's sacred solemnity

as if an orgy's
being held in a cathedral

light spirits
in masques of seriousness

between guffaws

the sublime
clown priest pronouncing
kyrie elieson

snickering

to those hidden
behind the high altar

then taken with
the profound holy aura

spinning from his words
in that glistening place

in the gladness
of reverent impulse

profaned

drops to his knees

splayed hands raised to heaven

Daniel Williams
Yosemite, CA

A ROOM OF ONE'S OWN

From the lone window she views the sugar
maples set ablaze in mid-October

where fields of asters and goldenrod grow with abandon
and two small boys play in the leaves in the distance.

The room holds a sturdy oak table burdened with papers
In a chair with goose-feathered cushion she leans

slightly forward, her gaze now drawn to the notes
scribbled last night on rough-textured paper.

Thoughts take form and shape. Like tasting fresh
strawberries in the bleak months of winter,

a hunger and delight of the soul. For this
all menial tasks around the home must wait.

Light pales with the sun's setting, Breaking
the silence, the scratching sound of her busy

pen and where the absorbing life of the mind
ventures onward till all light fades.

Irene K. Wilson
Lexington, MA

EXPERIMENTS WITH FOOD

When I first heard of the experiments my mother and step-father
made with food soon after they were married
I was an adolescent
trying to break free of their grasp
attempting to forge my own way
so the story did not interest me beyond the moment
as I thought how weird and unpleasant the combinations were

Today I think of them at the end of a busy day
at the store
opening kitchen cabinets
deciding what to combine

One day they mixed creamed corn and instant coffee
on another red meat and fruit and sardines

My mother said the combinations would never work
while my step-father hoped to happen on a miracle
something wonderful

Without recipes   without a guide
my parents were on their own
with only imagination to hold them back

The experiments continued as my step-father said,
"That's not quite right
It needs something more"
So he'd add whatever came to mind

Tonight he told me
"The trouble is the experiments never went far enough
I pick up the *Times* today and see combinations odder than ours"

Back in the middle 60's
They'd use anything in the cupboard
They still contend the meals were delicious
Today I think of them mixing and mixing
trying the varieties
hoping for a combination that would work

Laura Winters
Morristown, NJ

I AM TOO ALIVE TO BE OLD

"You must be bored, living alone,"
    say friends who analyze my life.
"You should get out and have some fun,"
    say relatives who understand me no more.
"What can you do with all your time?"
    say neighbors who should know better.

I may look old like the gray, winter
landscape, but I am too alive to be old.
    I laugh easily; I see clearly;
    I stopped focusing on the world's despair.
    I stopped trying to please everyone else.

    I live creatively; I live joyously.
    I love warmly and generously.
    I stopped judging others long ago.

I am too alive to be old.

E. Marie Woerner
Lincoln, NE

DANCING
(for Ben)

she to the he of the bountiful we
dance a dance, soft-stepping what is there,
together mimic not what is not there
the we shall see itself alone and free.

who shapes the seedy fellow of
seven edges and red clay stories;
a teller of tales on bitter words
and jealous wise to the living past

when were her sights placed on forever;
nimble and light though she was crafted
her passions weighed down her release,
the pain from a feather stifled her days

she sheds all smiles and carries
only the silent tunes
though hearing the stormy chorus
singing at Land's End.

he is marked a fire walker,
journeys far from all water signs;
the pursuit of everything under the sun
leads once again to the sun.

she to the he of the bountiful we.
the creation was in simple fashion
fevered empty nights, blind to the he and she;
bounty burst and carefree to the binding we.

Amy Wong
San Francisco, CA

REFLECTIONS ON MY FIRST AWAKENING

For a long moment we touched
Tender as dew drops nestled in the gentle
Folds of flowers
We planted and nurtured in our
Secret garden
Overlooking the crisp indigo waves
That now blanket and cradle the drowsy sun
Dully gleaming in my eyes as
I walk the waves in sleep
With salt water tears for our
Crinkled petals
Sprinkled in the endless deep
See

Laureen Wong
San Francisco, CA

OUT OF EDEN

We have fallen since that evening indeed;
you and I, Eve, we have fallen, saying
over in our hearts our cherished avowals.
So clasped by zeal, how could we know the law?
That night we had no answers for transgress
and journeyed in the desert that was cold,
longing for that we would not know again,
and had to invent clothes.

Moisture before, now dryness cakes my tongue.
No fresh thing drives me now. I look, then see
in eyes that vernal gleam—your longing, Eve.
What longing in me, too, there must still be!
I watch you wake to go forth at my side.
Because *I* did not know which fruit was which—
because *you* did not know which fruit was which—
we can't be damned for that!

We carry our direction out: faithful.
Your belly grows. I start to learn of joy
and anticipation. I learn of qualms:
fear of what it means, torments multiplied.
Not all the sons of ours can vanquish death,
injury and misfortune, sinful pride.
These acts we have no knowledge of forebode
and trouble m ind to sleep.

Weariness with our beauty coupling gives
vision to apprehension our race calls
fear, upon which we so foolishly act
avoiding it with acquired arts and sleights.
Wasn't it we, Eve, who built paradise,
two cells conspiring through the desert mold?
We were disgraced but triumph came of that!—
palms where we were expelled.

John Allen Young
Bakersfield, CA

WESTERN WIND!!

A force is felt, strong and penetrating
Heard by the lonely as the wind passes, devastating!
It's driving, bold; an emotional feeling
Love is the silent, longing, inward cry
Up from the ocean surface, salt spray reeling
The invisible passes, and utters a sigh.

Western wind, where do you come from?
Not all can see you, only some—
You bring rain, the life-blood of man,
To assert awesome power you swirl desert sand
Strong, powerful, yet compassionate and gentle
Universal master, is the emblem on your mantle.

Marilyn E. Yust
St. Charles, MO

NIGHT VISION

"It is all so ambiguous," she said.
"What is ambiguous," he asked,
"The scale and perspective."
"Of what"
"Of the windows. Those rectangles of windows."
"Where?"
"Look out there," she said. "High up. The lit windows over there."
"Frightening, isn't it?"
"Why," he asked.
"Because it's out there and not out there."
"Abstract and real."
"Windows in a sky that is not sky."
"Finitude that is infinity."
"Rubbish," he said.
"There are lights."
"There are windows
in a skyscraper."
"There is a sky."
"And it is night."

"Rubbish," she said.

Harriet Zinnes
New York, NY